Breaking Free From Financial Trauma

Dr. Nicole B. Simpson, CFP®

SPECIAL NOTE: To all corporations, universities, colleges, higher learning, religious, and professional organizations: Quantity discounts are available on bulk purchases of this book for educational, and gift purposes or as premiums for increasing magazine subscriptions or renewals. For additional information please contact **www.nicolebsimpson.com**

Dr. Nicole B. Simpson, CFP®

THIS IS A WRITTEN WORK BY
NICOLE B. SIMPSON
PUBLISHED BY HARVESTWEALTH PUBLISHING LLC

This is a book based on the divinely inspired thoughts of
Nicole B. Simpson.
All content therein was written as she recalled and recounted it.
All identities are used by permission or purposely omitted to protect the privacy of those living or dead.

Breaking Free From Financial Trauma
Copyright© August 2024
Nicole B. Simpson

Published in the United States of America by
Harvestwealth Publishing LLC 2024
An imprint of Harvestwealth Publishing LLC

All rights reserved under International Copyright Law. Contents and cover may not be reproduced in whole or in part in any form without the express written consent of the author(s) or publisher.

www.NicoleBSimpson.com

Library of Congress Cataloguing-In-Publication Number
PENDING

ISBN: 979-8-9871782-8-7

**First Edition Printing
Printed in the United States of America
August 2024**

Harvestwealth Publishing LLC
371 Hoes Lane Suite 200
Piscataway, NJ 08854

DEDICATION & SPECIAL THANKS

This book is dedicated to Abba Father who had more confidence in me than I had in myself. He knew I would stay the course and carry my cross.

I am grateful to every individual who took a chance with me when I established Harvest Wealth Financial in 2007. You trusted the vision and together we continue to soar!

I want to thank my sister Sonji K. Grandy who kept me afloat during the most traumatic financial season of my life.

Thank you, Ian Duhart, Dr. Angel Thompson and Crystal White, for helping me put Harvest Wealth Financial on the map.

Thank you, Legna Agency, for being the most amazing publishing partner.

Finally, thank you to Eugene L. Graves, Jr. who has committed his life to making sure I do not experience financial trauma ever again.

Dr. Nicole B. Simpson, CFP®

Dr. Nicole B. Simpson, CFP®

TABLE OF CONTENTS

Introduction	7
How Did We Get There	13
What Is Financial Trauma	19
The Money Pits	23
Emotions Versus Money	37
Charting A New Financial Path	45
Start Where You Are Standing	51
Establish Necessary Boundaries	61
Let Go of the Past	71
Commit to Staying Positive	75
Embrace Your New Normal	81
Build the Life You Desire	89
Stay The Course	97
About the Author	103

Dr. Nicole B. Simpson, CFP®

INTRODUCTION

I began this journey with a singular objective. That was to illuminate the real effects of financial trauma with the hopes that it resonates so deeply with my audience, that if they were stuck financially, it would shake them at the core. This book is written with the desire that you recognize all is not lost, and that the sense of dread when discussing money begins dissipating slowly. I also wanted to ensure that you understand I am not only writing as a textbook subject matter expert. I also lived this experience and that is why I know it is possible to break free from financial trauma.

So, I invite you to travel down this road with me as I engage you with testimonials and case scenarios you can identify with. I aim to connect with your emotions as you determine where you stand overall. For those who feel they are beyond the scope of what I am saying, that's wonderful to hear and you can celebrate your progress. I promise you will identify with the words that are flowing on these pages because breaking free from financial trauma takes time, it takes work. You may have navigated through rough emotional and economic terrain without a strategy or blueprint. That struggle is real. However, the lack of understanding about the relationship between the psychology of money and its influence on our financial decision-making is the culprit to financial dysfunction. Ignoring that connection causes many people to have cycles of stop-and-starts in their quest to become permanently financially free. Together we can establish a foundation that includes understanding financial patterns and their effect on your relationship with money. Stay with me!

Perhaps you are the first to graduate college. Your parents drilled in you that education was important if you wanted to grow up and become financially independent. They may not have used the words that connected finances with education because many households rarely discuss money. Those conversations remain virtually nonexistent. However, it could have translated that acquiring a sound education will help anyone get a great job and it positions you with opportunities to be successful. Maybe you knew since you were a little girl or boy what you wanted to do when you got older. You knew you loved working on cars, doing a friend's hair, sewing, journaling, or cooking. You dreamed of owning a salon or restaurant. For someone with talent, confidence flowed freely in your ability to perform, you understood that while the statistics were low for success, you believed in your athletic ability so much that you were going to make it as a professional. You strived to be in the Olympics, the NFL, or the NBA. You wanted to be the next Michael Phelps. It's also possible that you never did anything listed above, yet you simply wanted more. You may have felt that regardless of your childhood, you deserved an upgrade. You wanted a better life, a better hand than you had been dealt as a child. You wanted more opportunity, a chance to excel and go beyond the success or even challenges of your parents.

Growing up, you could have experienced a myriad of expectations regarding your future. And with everything within, you pursued different pathways, traveled many roads, and tried everything to make your dreams a reality. Now it is years, maybe even decades later and you find that you are standing in a place of full exhaustion, emotionally drained and you are not where you desired to be financially. Why? There has been a vicious cycle of pursuing your objectives and falling short. Each time you dared to dream again, start over, or pick up the plan, something obstructed your objectives.

After being in the wealth accumulation industry for over three decades, I have observed the significance of emotions and how they play a major role in our financial decisions. Oftentimes, when a person decides to develop a comprehensive life or financial plan, the focus remains on dollars and cents. A plan is created because you have filled out a questionnaire that asked you important questions such as when you would like to retire. Or how much money will you need to maintain a comfortable standard of living during retirement? How will you manage your final affairs, etc. etc. Lacking in the plan are several foundational questions that must be addressed if you want the plan to work. I like to connect them to the **"wh"** questions. Who, what, when where, and why.

Who are you creating the plan for? Who do you love enough to ensure that if you were permanently erased from the picture, if you died prematurely, if you were unable to work to contribute your fair share, the people you love will be fine financially? Who are you responsible for? In other words, who are the people relying upon you to take care of them? Do you have children, parents, or extended family members that you are their primary economic support system? The thing that can motivate you beyond your stagnation is oftentimes the people you love and desire to protect. When you look at them, you desire the best for them. It can also be for you. Sometimes we sacrifice ourselves in the most important areas of our lives. You should always plan for yourself first. When all else fails, you are responsible for your overall well-being; physically, mentally, emotionally, and economically.

What are your goals and objectives? I believe the 'what' question introduces us to the emotional relationship that can shape our financial lives. What do you want out of life? If you had the opportunity to ignore the need for financial support, what are your dreams, your aspirations? What would you like to be known for three or four generations beyond your lifespan? What legacy are you seeking to leave and how many people are important variables in your quest? When we begin to address what am I here for, it will eventually lead us to W-why, which I will leave for last.

When can be viewed in several ways. I can recall a study that stated when an individual is about to experience a milestone birth year, they make significant changes or adjustments in their lives the year prior to achieve stated goals. So, if someone always declared they wanted to purchase their first home by the age of 30, as they approach year 29, they seriously inquire about how to become a homeowner. The 'when' question can be a date or a certain timeframe. Children will often dream about what life will be like when they get older. Some even make declarations of what they are going to do the moment they become adults. In creating a plan, the question every advisor asks is simple, "When would you like to retire?" The moment when is defined, you can calculate financially how much you require in resources.

Where do you see yourself in one, five, ten, twenty years? Where is proximity. It is a place or position one desires to be at a certain interval. Building on the example stated in the "when" question, the arrival point is connected by the "where". That place is a house or being financially stable enough to afford being an owner instead of a tenant. It is a position of status that is ranked by socio-economic standards, educational standards, and influence. It guides your decisions as it points you toward where you are trying to land. Many individuals articulate where they desire to go but hesitate in making the actual plan. If you want to travel internationally, you must first secure a passport because where you are going, a passport is required. If you take the pressure of having to arrive somewhere in a set period, you will find that where you are going becomes easier to arrive. People are so accustomed to minimizing their timeline to complete a task. I have treasured the freedom of saying where I desire to be in decades, not years.

Why am I here? This question is both literal and figurative. Why are you in the place you are in now? Why did things happen in your lifetime and honestly, how did they contribute to your decision-making overall? Has your why crippled you into inaction? Does it cause you to remain stuck or afraid to confront it so much that you cannot move beyond the why? Before you respond, the question why isn't necessarily associated with taking any actions. It is asked more often, for an understanding or explanation of a particular issue. One may consider that asking the question why benefits your overall insight into how something may have transpired. But it doesn't necessarily prompt action. As you read this, there will be a moment where this book will prompt you to move beyond why into the place called how. When we arrive at that place, do not be afraid to take the first step. I am a firm believer that movement is a beneficial key. What happened to you was significant, yet it can only be crippling if you allow it to remain dominant. When we tackle why things transpired the way they did, it will open a door that I am hopeful you are willing to walk through.

There comes a moment in your life when you must own your place in this world. You will have to accept accountability for the choices you have made and that alone can be overwhelming. Those decisions were predicated upon the hand you were dealt, and you did not have enough information and/or understanding that led to additional options. We accept where you are standing now, but it is not the end of the road. Now we must decide what action items you are willing to implement because you are tired of the vicious cycle of stop and starts.

HOW DID WE GET HERE?

This book aims to help you navigate your life to determine if your financial decisions are based on emotional behavioral patterns learned as a child. Your upbringing is a great contributor to the choices you make financially. There is an adage that says, "Do as I say, not as I do." However, it isn't realistic. Children are extremely observant, and they mimic the behavior of their parents; what they say, how they live, and what they do. Therefore, if you grew up in poverty and experienced bouts of financial lack, it had a profound impact on your way of thinking. It showed up when food was scarce. Perhaps you came home from school and didn't have water, electricity or lights. Some individuals are familiar with not having a stable address and you moved from one school district to another too many times to count. In that instance, you may have become fixated on owning a house because you wanted stability when you were in control of your life. See how that shaped out? You began to design your life objectives based on your childhood experiences.

Identifying the memories of your childhood that contributed to how you see money is critical to breaking free. While family dynamics vary drastically, children learn from their environment. Are they exposed to a lifestyle of feasting or famine? For example, when payday or tax season rolled around, home life was festive, and things were positive. During the lean days, perhaps the days before payday, the attitudes of the adults surrounding you were terse at best. Because children are aware, they can see the patterns and identify good times versus the challenging days. This reality is not defined by poverty or confined to urban and rural areas. Regardless of one's socio-economic status, when a family lives from paycheck to paycheck, the threat of adopting practices that can lead to financial trauma is real.

We will not stop at determination and identification. Those are critical steps that lead to acceptance of what transpired. Once we begin to understand what is at the heart of your financial decision-making, we can strategically adjust to align your financial desires with your economic goals and objectives, while considering how you have operated in the past. The pathway will become more clearly defined because we can process the emotions while keeping the goal of breaking the shackles of poor choices that can hinder our progress. I have also found that taking this journey alone is possible, but less exciting. So, I suggest that you find an accountability partner that doesn't need to know the details of your monetary business but values you and they want to see elevation in your life. As you begin to implement strategies that will help you over time, that accountability partner can hold you to your affirmations. You will be free to disclose your journey based on your comfort level. Besides, you've heard the saying *your network reflects your net worth.* Doing great things can be contagious and you are going to want everyone connected to you to excel.

Finally, as a first-generation wealth accumulator, I am keenly aware of the pressure associated with being the financial foundation for your entire family, immediate and extended. While most will not verbalize it, such pressure is unfair and it's something that cannot be sustained over time without you eventually breaking. It's the primary reason why I am writing on such a difficult topic. As a practitioner, I built a book of business based on ordinary, everyday clients. They didn't have many assets, but through systematic investments and proper planning utilizing every financial tool available, my clients and I grew together. Over my almost twenty years in private practice, clients have gone back to school, established their businesses, risen in the corporate ranks, changed jobs for greater opportunities, and whatever else would help them achieve life goals.

This labor of literary love is my takeaway, and I am certain other professionals will add to or take away from my theory. Having said that, I must first disclose I am a woman of faith. I would not be who I am without divine guidance. While this book is not filled with spiritual affirmations, I must lay out what caused me to move forward more intentionally about addressing the connections between emotions and their influence on how people spend their money. After much prayer, I began to share in 2018 that people needed to focus on three areas. They needed to improve relations with their family, get their financial affairs in order, and stockpile food. I shared this message for over two years both via private channels and in public spaces, including social media. The last Wednesday in February 2020 on the 26th day, I was teaching Bible study, and I asked my congregation to stay online a bit longer because I wanted to reiterate my message with a greater sense of urgency. It was a simple short message, store up food and for those who just received large income tax refunds, do not be wasteful. Many of my clients share my faith and values and they followed my instructions.

Then came Covid-19 and it took a devastating toll on everyone. Those with greater means were able to withstand the pressures associated with not working and families across the country began to band together to address how this deadly disease was impacting them collectively. Children moved back home, grandparents were brought closer, and it wasn't unusual to find three generations living in proximity, or even in the same household. Everyone was coming together for survival's sake. During the height of Covid, drug and alcohol use increased, especially during the early stages of the pandemic. Online gambling became a common practice with an increased frequency causing many people to be at risk with a gambling addiction. As the world began to reopen, people returned to their normal lives but the family anchors, the reliable sources were left with invisible scars. Financial trauma was further exacerbated by extreme extenuating circumstances.

The pandemic took a serious toll on the world. Immediately, as we began to adopt a new normal, I began to observe a new level of financial anxiety. There were two extreme responses. As I toured the country speaking to thousands of people and engaging with my clients, I saw people who needed constant reassurance that they could withstand temporary financial picture.

The second thing was the people who admitted they avoided their financial standings because they didn't want to face how it impacted their overall financial standing. They thought not addressing the issue would make everything go away. Couple that with the reality that cabin fever was real. When the world reopened, people began to spend excessively to enjoy experiences. The death toll continued to rise, and it was being reported daily. The human attitude shifted and there was a universal opinion that life was short, tomorrow was not promised to anyone so everyone should enjoy the moment.

Look at the Taylor Swift and Beyonce craze. Ticket sales during their tours in 2023 were hundreds, if not thousands of dollars. People were seeking to go outside to create memories and have enjoyable experiences. They did whatever was necessary to pay for it, without considering the consequences in the future. But there would be a price to pay.

At the end of 2023, many first-generation wealth accumulators began to realize they needed to reset financially. What was a recurring sentiment? The historically reliable family bankers were struggling and when they were looking for reciprocation of the financial support they had always lent to their family and friends, they had no one to turn to. When they needed help, there was no one they could depend on. That reality was a wake-up call, and their emotions ran rampant. They saw that they were alone, and they could not rely on others economically while still being called on to be the financial anchor for those who could not help them during their moment of need. They had to process through the shame of being in a position where they needed help. They had to navigate through the guilt associated with their inability to provide support to their loved ones. They had to acknowledge their deep anger at feeling used and sometimes unappreciated. Finally, they had to face the reality that if they didn't provide for themselves, and did not set boundaries, their financial security would always be uncertain.

Financial trauma is real and while its definition is still being shaped, it is being defined through lived experiences. This will require professionals to understand how important it is to consider an individual's emotional connection with money before attempting to create a boilerplate plan that will never work. While it is the financial planner's job to help establish the plan, it cannot be based simply on what someone earns versus their expenses. Questions that include delving into an individual's financial history are critical. An assessment of spending patterns will reveal so much. Learning if a person is an emotional spender is necessary. Will a person sacrifice their financial well-being for the sake of their family? Most importantly, people must be asked the questions that help them learn if financial trauma is an issue for them. Several of those questions begin with these basic inquiries. Do you have any experiences such as job loss, the unexpected death of a primary wage earner, or a childhood of poverty that can influence your relationship with money?

WHAT IS FINANCIAL TRAUMA?

Approximately twenty-five years ago, I began to self-identify as a financial trauma expert. My justification at that time was perhaps a bit aspirational, at best. The truth is that I had endured some lived experiences that were traumatic, and I was dogmatically pursuing a methodology that I could implement that would help others rise out of poverty. It was my lived experiences coupled with my growing expertise in the financial planning arena, that helped me define it over the years. I was leaning on my actualized, verifiable expertise earned as a certified financial planner in October 2000. I offer this introduction as validation today because I have lived with this nuanced reality, even when it was not clearly defined or acknowledged.

So, what is financial trauma? I define it as the challenges people experience when they cannot cope with or process the reality that they have inadequate financial resources or perhaps they have encountered a significant and/or abrupt financial loss. The definition of trauma is when one experiences something extremely stressful, frightening, or distressing. It can be one experience or a series of events that are difficult to cope with or it may be something outside of one's control. In my own life, I experienced trauma growing up in a physically and sexually abusive household. That was a series of events over an extended period. I was also on the 73rd floor of 2 World Trade Center on September 11th, 2001. That traumatic experience was a one-time incident. Financial trauma is the same engagement as one evaluates their financial status. It is real, while not clinically defined. Leaders in the financial services field and mental health field have begun to explore the relationship between people and their money and recognize there is an intersection between the two.

Living in poverty is stressful. The anxiety associated with one's inability to pay for the essentials necessary to function seamlessly can impact the mental state of any individual. The despair that engulfs a person when they have a lack of resources can cause people to make poor decisions that further exacerbate the issue, rather than resolve it. Think for a moment about a single mother with three children who is already struggling to survive. Consider how that family will be greatly impacted by an untimely illness of a child or an unexpected school closure. The mother is forced to miss work or pay someone to care for her children during her absence. The added expense or loss of income can devastate the mom who was already working hard to make ends meet.

There was a time when individuals couldn't identify with poverty, or better yet, they didn't know they were poor. You may be familiar with the narratives passed down from generation to generation. Your elders would share what life looked like growing up. As a Generation Xer, someone born between 1965 and 1980, I recall the Baby Boomer generation (1946-1964) always saying how they didn't know they were poor when they grew up. They thought it was simply a way of life. However, their environment began to shift so dramatically, that it became apparent there was a common denominator between them and the people surrounding them. One notable shift was the emergence of housing projects. In 1935, because of the New Deal, the first housing project in Atlanta, GA, named the Techwood Homes, was constructed. The New Deal was enacted by President Franklin D. Roosevelt to help rescue the U.S. from the Great Depression. When established, the project evicted hundreds of black families to create the 604 unit, whites-only neighborhood.

While Techwood Homes was the first housing project, it quickly became a reality that the most economically challenged families, regardless of their ethnicity, gravitated to government-funded housing developments because they offered income-subsidized low rents. People without an income and the working poor all clustered together struggling financially from day to day. The single mother with three children oftentimes lived in such a place trying not only to survive, but also to find a way out of those conditions. These conditions created urban areas, where poverty existed and the housing quarters were hazardous and unclean, employment was scarce or if someone found a job, it certainly did not reflect a sustainable living wage. Finally, the housing projects were outright dangerous. Alcoholism and substance abuse remain prevalent in the 21st century and not much has changed from Techwood Homes to every urban city, USA today.

On the flip side, rural poverty is equally devastating. Some characteristics of rural poverty are that the family size tends to be larger and their primary ability to earn is through the agricultural sector. Because the land is generally underdeveloped, access to essentials can be difficult. Grocery markets are a great distance, wireless connectivity is erratic, and schools are not as easily accessible as in the ghetto. The infrastructure in rural areas is so egregious, things people in the ghetto take for granted are precious commodities in an average rural area.

Dr. Nicole B. Simpson, CFP®

THE MONEY PITS

Financial lack is a primary cause of financial trauma. Children who grow up in abject poverty have been exposed to major financial drama that can confuse an individual when trying to learn proper money management. Two major annual seasons that contribute to the chaos and misguided perceptions about money are Christmas and tax season time. Both times create an illusion in many households that all is well financially. A Christmas tree that is adorned with beautiful ornaments, presents surrounding the base of the tree and so much food for one day that is spread across the table with delightful treats that appear to be enough to feed the entire neighborhood. It is set up like a wonderful feast fit for a king or like grandma's house on Thanksgiving Day.

Weeks after Christmas comes tax season time. When someone with children files their taxes and they are considered the working poor, they can potentially receive a tax refund that can equal two months' salary. Yet instead of saving that money and using it systematically to improve their quality of life all year, families will purchase high-priced items such as a car, new furniture, or a new television. Some people will even go on a vacation they cannot afford without that refund. Let me break it down.

If a mother of two received a refund of $4500, the family would benefit more if the mom put the money in an interest-bearing account and withdrew $300 each month to help her with her expenses. That amount can improve the entire family's standard of living and incrementally, they can begin to create a plan of action that can help them improve their quality of life over time.

Any person can improve their financial status as they grow older and begin working, even if they grew up poor. As an adult, you are in control of your destiny and the first lesson you must master is that regardless of your income, you must adopt a healthy mindset or attitude towards money. Even individuals who begin to earn a high income must implement a strategic plan because one's mindset doesn't adjust to an influx of resources. Unfortunately, just because you are making a decent wage doesn't mean you have proper money management skills. A disconnect appears in unconscious ways. For example, now you can afford to go on vacation.

After all, you work hard all year long and you have planned the trip for quite some time. You budgeted for everything, and you even picked the days based on your closest payday. You promised yourself that you would not spend anything beyond the funds you allocated for your vacation. Everything is going according to plan until you are on that beach, in the casino, or walking through the streets of a country you have always wanted to visit. While you are there, your impulses are to spend what you can afford. Does that stop you since you see the amount in your checking account? No! You immediately decide you deserve to be happy and to treat yourself well. After all, you work hard, and you will figure things out when you get home!

Being subjected to financial abuse is financial trauma. It is identified as a tactic the perpetrator will use on a partner they desire to control or manipulate. It involves limiting their partner's access to resources, demanding they come to the abuser for access to money, or simply keeping the victim in the dark regarding the family finances. When the dominant partner does not allow the victim to know much about the financial position of the family, the victim is subject to financial abuse, and it can be quite traumatizing. I can recall my first conversation with a longstanding client. Already divorced, but still living with her ex-spouse, her goal was to move out and be free from his influence. He had convinced her that she did not have adequate resources without him. After one review, I convinced her she could pack up and leave whenever she desired. She was so manipulated that she had no idea what she had accumulated over time. She was both the victim of financial abuse and traumatized. We were able to create a strategic plan that made sense to her. At the same time, I had to be sensitive to triggers that caused her to be anxious about her future.

My experience with this client allowed me to see beyond dollars and cents. On paper, she could have retired whenever she desired. But because she was led to believe she would be impoverished without her mate; she carried the fear of running out of money. She liked to shop and purchase expensive items. The best way to ease her concern was NOT to use the word budget but to provide her with an allowance that was more than she needed. The one thing I observed during the data gathering, was her desire to "create events". Therefore, understanding she enjoyed excursions helped me to craft a budget that she would accept. The figure appeared quite high and beyond her typical spending habits, but the amount offered would never negatively impact her standard of living and it helped ease her anxiety. Based on candid conversations, I realized how important it was for her to have access to money to do things she desired. Once she became secure with the truth of knowing she was financially free, she moved forward comfortably, breaking the chains of financial bondage that held her hostage for so many years.

This is the introduction to understanding the benefits of recognizing the psychology of money and how people see it, matters. My engagement with her showed me that the trauma was real, even if the reality of the experience was no longer applicable. Dealing with someone's emotions as they relate to money through recognizing their pattern of behavior is essential for a breakthrough. Think about someone who is deemed successful in their vocation. They are a highly compensated employee or a successful entrepreneur, yet they "feel" they are struggling and lacking. Much of their philosophy has been shaped by historical experiences. To dismiss it will cause anyone trying to help to be ineffective.

Identification of the issue isn't sufficient. Pointing out a person's financial insecurities without presenting a possible resolution doesn't erase the matter. It is critical to engage honestly and critically about a person's spending habits before attempting to both analyze and adjust. How does one begin to understand the patterns? A perfect way to paint a picture is to review someone's primary bank statement for a period of three to six months. Combing through the monthly activity provides insight. For example, if you are going to Walmart or a grocery store one or two times weekly and you are spending $150 to 200 dollars, what are you buying? Are you using the trip to the store as an ATM? Are you buying a few necessary items and then withdrawing the remainder in cash? If so, what are you doing with the cash?

Another way to critically assess one's attitude toward money is to consider how a person operates when they are seeking to relax and rest. Is a night out on the town your idea of relaxation? Do you enjoy dinner and a movie or doing something with consistency that has a price tag? To relax is to be free from stress, anxiety, and tension. Many people consider a vacation as an outlet for rest and relaxation. Therefore, how someone plans a vacation versus how they operate once they get there matters. Many people plan their activities in advance. Do you stick to the budget you set for yourself, or do you spend money without consideration that the result of your behavior will compromise you financially when you return home? Another consideration is something I noticed years ago. How many people need a vacation from the vacation? In the excitement of going somewhere outside of your normal environment, you plan for every moment you are away. That alone is exhausting because you have done everything EXCEPT rest and/or relax. Now you have returned home, and you have spent more money than you intended. You will say it was worth it because you created memories. The memories are great indeed, but the goal is still to achieve the initial objective of resting and staying within your budget moving forward.

The loss of resources, going from the place of plenty to struggling is another cause of financial trauma. This can appear when there is an unexpected and significant financial loss that is difficult to recover from immediately. For example, on August 29, 2005, Hurricane Katrina devastated the city of New Orleans, a city that was already economically vulnerable. Before the hurricane, it was lagging behind other large American cities in the labor force participation rates and employment-to-population ratios. The city was able to avoid a direct hit, but the levee system failed causing the city to be flooded. Over 1 million people evacuated, but those who did not have the resources were stuck in their homes and/or designated shelter areas. In addition to the actual loss, the challenge was further exacerbated due to poor rescue efforts and the government's inability to provide emergency food and other necessary items because they were dealing with hazardous conditions. The storm caused over $150 billion in damages and the working poor suffered in incalculable ways.

Tragic things happen. Natural disasters, mass shootings, personal horrors. The aftermath of Hurricane Katrina highlighted how a traumatic event can have a great and devastating effect. People lost everything and then had to contend with insurance companies and agencies whose mission statements declared they were available to help displaced people suffering. Unfortunately, how does one produce documents to prove their personal property? When filing a claim, an adjuster is generally dispatched to assess the damages. What needs to be repaired externally and what was housed within? In New Orleans, there wasn't anything to assess. Therefore, companies calculated an amount that was significantly below the loss and people who were already struggling were not made whole financially. Now they are without a home, many lost their jobs, and the money received reflected a fraction of their loss. They were subjected to financial trauma.

Unemployment is another major factor. Since the turn of the century, I can recall three periods where Americans saw mass unemployment and the response was economic anxiety. What many people do not realize is that America was already in the middle of a recession that had rising unemployment when the tragedy of September 11th, 2001, occurred. It further exacerbated the recession that began in March 2000 due to the dot.com bust. Thereafter, when the World Trade Center and the Pentagon were attacked, it added an additional layer of anxiety that reverberated throughout the world. The financial mecca of the world was targeted, and terrorists made every effort to bring the country to its knees. At the same time, families were dealing with loss of life because 2,996 people died and thousands more walked away chronically ill. Many could not work. Not every survivor who was chronically ill was impacted by unemployment. They may have collected disability or worked through their injuries. The latter was the case for me. I didn't even know I was entitled to workman's compensation until a decade had passed. Those who worked for temporary agencies and independent contractors were unemployed overnight. However, regardless of the classification, many survivors' financial lives were significantly altered. The actual unemployment numbers were revised from 4.95% unemployment to 5.79%, which represented a rise of 0.84%.

The second shared experience of rising unemployment occurred during what has been identified as The Great Recession of 2008. It started in December 2007 and hit the bottom in 2009. To understand this impact, one must review the housing market's rise and ultimate fall. It was a great contributor to the severity of the impact of unemployment. When a family does not have housing security, it will affect their overall well-being. So, to understand the connection, one must know that since the 1990s, the housing market expanded greatly, and home prices and home ownership increased at record levels. After the 2001 recession ceased, interest rates that were reduced to fight the recession during that period remained in place so borrowing became much easier. Home ownership became possible for lower-income individuals because of all the housing initiatives that were established to attract new buyers. The down payment for first-time homeowners was decreased substantially, making the process more affordable. In addition, programs were established for people who were historically deemed a poor credit risk. In other words, people who had a poor credit history, low income, or no credit at all were now offered a program that allowed them to make a smaller deposit on a home, borrow money at lower interest rates, and with the government's assistance, secure a mortgage. Lenders began to offer mortgages and then repackage them in the early 2000s into securities investments.

The greater demand for housing increased the supply and it was reflected in the numbers. Many of the new jobs that were created during that same time were in housing-related sectors. Initially, things were positive as the value of property in the United States doubled between 1998 and 2008, making it one of the largest increases in history. But as Isaac Newton infamously stated, "What goes up, must come down." Housing prices began to peak in early 2007 and when that occurred, the subprime loans that were turned into investments began to drop substantially. As the demand for housing construction dried up and layoffs ensued, the borrowers who were already a high credit risk, began to default on their loans and the mortgage-related assets crashed. The financial service industry was affected, and once solid, reputable institutions vanished virtually overnight. Two major institutions were Bear Stearns, which was acquired by JP Morgan Chase, and Lehman Brothers which filed for bankruptcy. It didn't stop there. AIG, a large insurance company needed the Federal Reserve's financial support to stop the hemorrhaging.

People were losing their homes and their jobs. The federal government bailed out major corporations at the expense of the American people, but the people still suffered financially and that was a secondary contributor to the financial trauma that exists. If I can make a connection to the impact of September 11th, I think one would get an even clearer picture.

It took years for people to understand the consequences of that tragedy. Now first responders and World Trade Center survivors were experiencing medical challenges that hindered their ability to earn. Medical experts initially did not consider what would be the long-term affects emotionally, physically, and economically. People did not recover in six years so when the housing crisis emerged, those people who were barely holding on, were devastated yet again.

Let me draw the connection on a personal level. In the immediate aftermath of September 11th, my income dropped from earning over $100,000 to less than $20,000 the following year. I was a new homeowner, having purchased my house in September 1999. I worked on the 73rd floor of Two World Trade Center and I was in the building, still on the 44th floor when Tower II was hit. In addition to the loss of income, I was physically affected. I could not breathe. I could not sleep and was having nightmares whenever I did. As a certified financial planner, I didn't get the help or support from anyone in the industry. As previously stated, I didn't know I qualified for workman's compensation. In hindsight, I do understand that everyone was struggling, and communication was horrid. At the same time, I was not a first responder. So, when the reports began to emerge that comparable chronic illnesses were impacting the first responders, their medical challenges sounded familiar. Eventually, it was evident that people who were exposed to the toxic fumes on September 11th could experience various illnesses. I was eventually diagnosed with asthma, COPD, anxiety, and PTSD. I was medically deemed permanently, and partially disabled.

I can attest firsthand to the anxiety and struggles I endured trying to save my home. At the same time, my income did not recover in the third, fourth or even fifth year. Yes, it increased incrementally, after such a significant drop, but that is something many displaced workers can validate. When faced with unemployment, people are forced to take a new job, and the salary may decrease. Because you need to work, you cannot afford to pass up an offer. So now, if you were already struggling from day to day, your anxiety has increased significantly. As a homeowner, expenses are unpredictable. Taxes can increase, a leak in a faucet can occur, the utility costs can rise. Anything can happen and affect your expenses from day to day. You are responsible for the maintenance of your home. The feeling is comparable to a slow leak on a ship. You feel yourself going under and you are making every effort to stay afloat, fighting, kicking, clawing. Yet the feeling is inevitable. You dread what lies ahead because you know you are losing the war. That feeling is real.

It was reported that between October 2008 and April 2009, the loss of jobs monthly averaged 700,000. The research supports my assertion that people who did find new jobs did earn significantly less, and their overall quality of life was altered. Many suffered from foreclosure, and they lost all their equity in their homes. They were forced to find new housing arrangements much like the victims of Hurricane Katrina. They were left to rebuild with fewer resources and now they have a worse credit history.

Finally, the world came to a literal halt due to the worldwide pandemic of 2020. Since the bottoming of the Great Recession of 2008, the financial recovery for families steadily rose. At the end of 2019, the labor market was extraordinarily hot, and unemployment was at historic lows. Then in the Spring of 2020, when it was fully understood how dangerous Coronavirus was. Mass layoffs had occurred in February and March of that year. At first, they were temporary with April

2020's number coming in with unemployment at 14.8%. Then President Donald J. Trump signed the Cares Act, which was a $2.2 trillion economic stimulus bill. One of the benefits of that act was the Paycheck Protection Program. It authorized the Small Business Administration to create and distribute a loan guarantee program that would assist companies with resources to stay open. Since the government shut the country down, things like payroll and nondiscretionary expenses still needed to be paid. What made it unique is that all eligibility entities included self-employed and independent contractors in addition to the traditional corporations, small businesses, non-profit organizations and others.

This season of unemployment was arguably disproportionate and very emotionally draining. Families had to deal with unexpected deaths, loss of permanent income of primary wage earners, and the fact that the disease was so contagious. Women, especially single parents, struggled to find the balance between caring for their young children and the need to work. Anyone unable to manage both was the first to be terminated. A secondary factor was that they were primary caregivers for their elderly parents. According to the Centers for Disease Control and Prevention, the numbers landed at 350,831 victims in 2020, 415,000 in 2021, and in May 2022, one million people had died. It was the elderly who were at the greatest risk. The emotional turmoil and the uncertainty of death and/or disability reverberated throughout the country.

Not everything can be classified as financial trauma. However, poverty, loss of resources or unemployment, and financial abuse rank high in definition. While the list has not been fully exhausted here, I do want to address one additional cause and that is increasing debt. Debt is defined as something that is owed or due, typically money. The uneasiness of increasing debt is understandable because it comes with signing contracts with a lot of words. Think about it. If you are going to college, the paperwork is both long and confusing. It contains language that doesn't make sense, but because you know it's the only way you can achieve your pursuit of higher education, you hold your breath and sign promissory notes.

The worst kind of debt, in my opinion, is credit card debt. While it is the worst, it can be relatively easy to attain. At the beginning stages of my speaking career, I visited many college campuses. This is how I see it. At the beginning of the year, young, impressionable kids are targeted. How? In front of the average student center are tables filled with your school's memorabilia. Everyone wants their school's sweatshirt or bookbag, something that reflects you belong. As you peruse the table, you inquire about the cost and the representatives indicate it's free…if you sign up for a credit card. You think little of it and you sign on the line so you can enjoy the temporary gratification of getting a nice sweatshirt. Weeks later, a credit card appears in the mail, right before your scheduled freshman party. How is it possible that you qualified for a credit card with a part-time campus job if you have one? But now, you have access to credit, and this is the perfect opportunity to get that slamming outfit that will make you known on campus. At first, you manage the credit effectively until you hit midterms, and you can't work because school is your priority. Slowly the credit limit increases until your payments become unsustainable. Unfortunately, some people fall into the trap of getting multiple cards and before you know it, it's out of control. So, what do you do? You decide you will figure it out later in life, like when you graduate.

The ritual of purchasing a house and a car is similarly overwhelming. While the process is different, both charge an interest rate per your creditworthiness. So, you may not get declined when seeking to purchase a car. However, you will be charged an interest rate that is based on what the company deems your credit risk is worth. If it appears that you have the ability and the history reflects you can repay the loan, your interest rate is lower. If you have the ability from an income perspective, but your history shows that you have missed a few payments or you have a late payment history, it doesn't mean that you will not be granted the loan. However, you will be penalized with a higher interest rate since you have been identified as a credit risk. Putting it all together, if you have student loan debt, an outstanding mortgage, or credit card debt and you are financing a car, you may feel the stress associated with that heavy weight.

One final note regarding debt and liabilities. Sometimes you may feel pressured into co-signing for a loved one. It means that you are guaranteeing the debt will be paid. Therefore, if someone asks you to cosign for a car, you are telling the finance company that if the benefactor of the car does not pay the monthly obligation, you are ready to assume the responsibility. I'm not certain if people understand the gravity associated with guaranteeing you will pay for something you will not have the primary benefit of utilization. You have been asked because your income may be higher, or your credit may be better. Be careful of who you are signing for. As a practitioner, I understand it may cause issues between you and your family members. In most cases, I caution my clients against it, looking for other solutions, especially if my clients are hell-bent on helping their families out. Sometimes an outright gift or loan to the party in need proves to be helpful to both parties. With a car, a higher down payment can get someone across the line to purchase the vehicle independently. Other requests have been for furniture and even a house.

Since I mentioned the house, couples may have encountered this issue. You are together and ready to move forward in the relationship and purchase property. One person has excellent credit and income high enough that they qualify individually. The second party has good credit and a reasonable income but is weighed down by student loans and a brand-new car. Adding them would negatively impact your ability to secure a loan because their debt-to-income ratio may be underwater or upside down. Or they may have property because of a previous relationship. If you are married the loan officers may suggest that you take out the loan, but the other party is still able to have their name added to the deed. When in love, everything is fine. But what if the relationship turns sour? You are responsible for the mortgage, and they are entitled to interest in the home if everything is not structured properly. If you are married, the structure does not matter. The general rule is that property acquired during marriage and used as the primary residence is joint property. The pressure of assuming that debt can lead to financial trauma.

The examples listed are daily occurrences that can cause great apprehension when addressing financial status and responsibility. Whatever may cause someone to endure such trauma, there is a way to face it directly and break free. Now that we have defined it, let's address the strategic solutions.

EMOTIONS VERSUS MONEY

Thinking about money and its control over human decisions is very powerful. The correlation between someone's attitude toward their finances and how they live matters. It is the primary reason why exploring the meaning of life beyond the need for money is a helpful exercise. A great way to begin is simple. If money wasn't an issue, what would you do? What would be your purpose in life? Would you have the courage to pursue a goal or a dream? The best way to confront financial trauma is to consider how having money or the lack of resources has defined you. You have adopted behavioral patterns over the years, and they originated from somewhere. Did you rob Peter to pay Paul because you lived from paycheck to paycheck and what you brought home was never enough? Did the concept of feast or famine resonate with you? When financial times were good, you partied hard and celebrated. Yet when the money was scarce, in addition to realizing your attitude was different, you struggled and maybe even felt a little depressed.

If you never saw your parents pay a bill, work on a budget, or even have money conversations, you were left to figure out its use for yourself. Sure, you grew up asking your parents to buy you something when you went to the store. Some days you got what you asked for, and other days you were disappointed they said no. I believe it affects you. I can give you an example. Growing up, Christmas was rarely celebrated in my house because money was extremely scarce. My family was deemed working poor. In other words, my mom earned too much to be classified as poor and receive government benefits, yet not enough to cover the day-to-day expenses. If you add any alcoholism or drug addictions to the mix, something that was rampant in the projects, it could be a primary factor in why people didn't have enough resources. For us, the end of the month was extremely rough, and you could tell the struggle was real based on what was being served for dinner. For many years during the holiday season, we barely had gifts as a young, impressionable child. When I say little, one year I received a pair of glitter socks as my only gift. Not a doll, not a book- socks with glitter. There were times when we received nothing. Making matters worse, a major school activity was to write a letter to Santa. The teacher would make certain it would make it to the North Pole. That added pressure made kids like me think even Santa didn't care about me. I learned early that Santa was not real, and that we were poor!

Holding onto those memories and allowing them to shape what you do as an adult sounds silly, right? However, think about how you *felt* as a little child. As you grew older and you secured your first job, what did you do during the holiday seasons? Did you purchase gifts for everyone you knew? Did you buy yourself everything you desired? Did you spend more money than anticipated? Equally important, now that you are a parent think about your first Christmas in your new role. Your child is less than 1 year old and you're thinking about what to purchase and the baby doesn't know a thing about the holiday. It means absolutely nothing to them, but something within you was possibly triggered. You were thinking about how you felt as a child and you projected your emotions. You were going to make sure your children never felt that sense of sadness, even if you went into debt until tax season approached.

This was my reality. I was a teenage mom, and my eldest son was born in March 1990. Therefore, he was 9 months old when his first Christmas came. I promise you; he had no clue about the significance of Christmas and for his first holiday, the house looked like a toy store invaded my small apartment. In retrospect, it was ridiculous because I spent over $1000 to compensate for my lack when I was a child. It was not logical, and I could not control myself. I can vividly recall fighting against the fear of my childhood. Why am I sharing this? I was operating out of pure emotions, not logic. At the same time, I cannot honestly say that I've overcome those emotions either. What I did manage to do is channel my energy into a more productive space, while making adjustments that take into consideration my perspective and the emotional roller coaster of the holiday season. I have my reasons why.

Earlier, I mentioned my personal connection to the tragedy of September 11th. My family and several close friends had just established a nonprofit organization earlier in the year to help marginalized and oppressed people by elevating their voices. People were not being heard in our local community. After the tragedy, we shifted slightly the agenda of the organization. Several national organizations raised millions of dollars at that time to assist people who were devastated by the tragedy. Initially, I did not seek out their support because I was so grateful to be alive. However, after serious prompting from my colleagues, I broke down and went to seek help. The experience was one of the most devastating and embarrassing experiences of my life. I was stripped of my dignity and that feeling left me broken and full of despair. I was treated as if I was a second-class citizen. The organization did not express empathy for what I endured; it was horrid. I vowed to do whatever I could to help struggling families during financial dark times. One of the first acts of the organization was to provide holiday gifts to families who were identified as the working poor; people who were like my mother as I was growing up.

My childhood experience still shapes how I serve during the holiday season. It also helps me to determine who we want to target. The reason why is that I am trying to help a young child by protecting them from feeling what I felt. The experiences of my past not only linger in my consciousness but also affect how I behave today. In these moments, the memories do not die. They are the catalysts for why you operate the way you do presently. That cannot be dismissed. This is why acknowledgment of those moments must be considered. It will help you to move forward. This does not mean you will ignore or must fight against your history. However, recognizing its existence and its contribution to how you think can offer a level of understanding when evaluating your spending patterns.

I believe the industry has taken an approach to financial planning based on data input, projected rates of returns, and what should work if someone follows the plan. It does not account for deviations or periods of irrational spending. For those who advertise that they take a holistic, customized approach, something is almost always off. If we seriously desire to advance financial stability on a major scale, we must seek out the connection between one's financial behavior and their plan. The goal isn't always to change how you operate because it's bad or problematic. The goal is to identify why something causes you to stray from a carefully constructed financial plan. The goal is to recognize what is causing you to spend money you don't have. Then you can process how you want to move forward after identification. Sometimes one can change that behavior and then there are moments where you must include it into the plan in a healthier, more constructive way.

I can recall meeting an individual who was the favorite aunt in her family. She didn't have children, so she spoiled her nieces and nephews as they were growing up. She was successful and had come from a relatively large family. Quickly, she became the family banker whenever a financial crisis arose. At first, she experienced a great sense of appreciation that she could be there for her family. However, the family began to expect her financial support for other events such as milestone birthday parties, family reunions, and weddings. The outside pressure was both emotionally and financially draining and she didn't have the bandwidth to say no. It was her childhood memories that made her suppress her emotions and remain silent. Unfortunately, how she interacted with her family began to reveal there was a problem brewing. She felt they only valued her when she would pay for something they wanted or needed. In addition, they rarely communicated just to see how she was doing. She would engage them while displaying an attitude and great resentment.

The resentment and feeling unappreciated aren't unusual. No one wants to disappoint their family, nor do they want to feel taken advantage of. It does place things into perspective. You begin to ask yourself questions that are difficult to address. It can create insecurity and uncertainty regarding how others see you. At the same time, you're seeking more for yourself. You recognize that if you want to break the cycle of lack, you must make difficult decisions that may disappoint others. I would offer you this. When someone is riding on an airplane, before every ride, the flight attendants will repeat over the intercom that if you are traveling with other passengers and an emergency arises, you must first secure your mask before you attempt to assist anyone else. It does not matter how often you travel, that message is conveyed before takeoff on every flight. This is critical in securing your financial foundation as well. It can prove to be a dangerous proposition trying to save someone else financially when you have not secured your safety. Where is your lifeline and who is willing to help you?

I recognize that implementing a plan that puts you first can be easier said than done. Just as Rome was not built in a day, shifting may take time and adjustments. You are not going to cut your loved ones off, but you do need to ensure that helping them does not hurt you. The favorite aunt understood she needed to pivot. She was willing to have the difficult conversations to set things in order. At the same time, she increased her emergency cash allocation to ensure that if the family had a significant emergency, she would be in a position to help. Since she was committed to her financial stability, she invited her family to meet with her financial planner for a social event that she called her "Financial Freedom" day. Turning a family outing into a financial literacy educational day of learning was brilliant. The aunt set up games and prizes that were carefully crafted to educate and empower. Throughout the day, she outlined her vision for herself and what she desired for others. She ended the day with a question-and-answer session that she titled, "Ask the Expert." Throughout the day, she was intentional about sharing with her family that she needed to set boundaries so the entire family could benefit.

The aunt's approach was innovative, and she enlisted the support of professional associates because she was committed to getting herself on the right track financially. It was also a rare response to a real issue that haunts many seeking to manage their affairs effectively. When confronted with the choice of fight or flight, in the financial realm, flight is typically the first option until something so drastic occurs that people are forced to change. It's almost like having a near-death experience. Well, not that drastic but it has been defined as the physiological reaction one has when they are stressed or frightened. The cause of the threat activates the sympathetic nervous system and triggers a response that says stay and work through the issue or run away from the issue. The aunt navigated through her challenges, while many people continue to push the issue down the road financially until they can no longer prolong the matter. Usually, the latter response makes a bad situation even worse, and the consequences tend to be more dire.

CHARTING A NEW FINANCIAL PATH

Today financial planners, investment advisors, and mental health counselors are acknowledging that one cannot ignore the connection between the psychology of money and how it affects people emotionally. Financial professionals are seeking to understand the mindset and attitude of their prospective clients before recommending someone implement a portfolio with great or minimal risk. I believe we are moving in the right direction. At the same time, we have much more work to do, especially after surviving the global pandemic. Dealing with so much death and despair, coupled with financial anxiety has become a heavy weight in the lives of so many. Take a moment to consider its impact on your life. Were you in school and had to go home to complete your education via Zoom? While I am much older than that demographic, I completed my doctorate in December 2019. My graduation was supposed to be in May 2020 and there was no graduation ceremony. I felt robbed of a milestone accomplishment. Couple that with the fact that I turned 50 years old in January 2021 and felt cheated even more.

Covid had a major impact, something comparable to the effects of death, and death is devastating enough. For the families directly affected by the death of a loved one and for single-parent households specifically, they were more detrimentally hindered financially. Let's unpack the impact based on a real-life scenario. The loss of revenue to the family created greater economic instability. If the person who succumbed to Covid was a financial contributor to the household, their income can no longer be relied upon. This is true, even if the deceased was on a fixed income. Therefore, if there was a family of five in a household and one of the family members was the grandmother to the children and she transitioned during Covid, her income was removed from the monthly budget. If the household was three adults, the impact could be minimal. However, what if the family dynamics were a mother of three children and a grandmother? Now, in addition to the loss of income, childcare is also a challenge. The surviving adult had to figure out how to make sure the children remained safe and received their education via Zoom, and she still had to work. This was during the time that people were forced to stay home and not travel outside of the home unless they were deemed essential workers.

Dealing with the actual death meant trying to grieve the loss of a loved one while preparing funeral arrangements that were not traditional. One could acknowledge that the actual funeral is a necessary component of the grieving process, a final goodbye, a way to mark the life and legacy of the deceased. During that time, The Center for Disease Control issued guidelines that needed to be strictly adhered to which limited attendance to the actual funeral. People implemented technology into the services so that others could join virtually to support immediate family and close friends. In addition to wearing face masks, social distancing was necessary as well. If the deceased person's cause of death was COVID, additional restrictions were applied such as no touching, wrapping, or dressing of the body, no kissing, and careful handling of the personal belongings was critical. Even the ceremony or rituals were impacted by the elimination of traditional music and words from attendees to reduce the possible flow of saliva through the air. These conditions heightened the bereavement experience and left many people directly profoundly impacted.

After the funeral was the settling of the estate and in addition to the income loss, the final affairs still required management. At this time, the world was operating with skeleton personnel. Things that were seamless to navigate became difficult and time-consuming. The first step would be to retrieve a death certificate, which was secured by the funeral home. Many funerals were delayed for weeks, causing great financial hardship because families did not have access to the money of the decedent. For a family living from paycheck to paycheck, a month could create significant financial chaos. Once the death certificate was secured, anything deemed a will substitute could be retrieved by the named beneficiary. A will substitute is something that passes directly to the beneficiary and it bypasses probate. Any retirement money, insurance policies, and accounts that have a payable on death option are considered will substitutes. It allows people faster and easier access to funds.

Before the pandemic, one could simply visit their local county clerk's office and request time with the surrogate court to have a will probated. This process is simply the validation of the decedent's final wishes. The County Surrogate will authenticate the will; usually the original will and not a duplicate copy. It will also give the authorization paperwork to the executor of the estate who will need to manage the final affairs. During Covid, the process became more stringent. Initially, the courts were closed across the country, while deaths were increasing significantly. Keep in mind that people were not just succumbing to Covid, regular issues were still transpiring and lack of care because of Covid caused deaths as well. You may have heard of the people who died of cardiac arrest or strokes and other life-threatening issues, because of the strain Covid placed on the healthcare system.

When the courts finally reopened, there was a serious backlog, and everything was transferred to process documents online. In addition to facing the rising death tolls, the workload was overwhelming. Original wills and death certificates still needed to be mailed, making a bad situation worse. For many families, the death was unexpected and planning had not even been considered. The same mother of three who had to bury her mother in the middle of COVID-19 would have struggled to get appointed as the executor or personal representative if the mother did not have her affairs in order. How does that impact her standard of living?

It is most unfortunate that women carried the burden or greater weight during the pandemic. In addition to being strong for their children, they were the most likely class of people who were primary caregivers to their parents. Those same women were great financial contributors to the maintenance of the house. I can recall reading an article that addressed the elevated stress and anxiety of being overwhelmed and lonely simultaneously. They suffered financial and material hardships and were the most susceptible to job loss. This harsh reality was a tipping point for many families who decided they needed to take personal accountability for where they were standing financially and they began to reach out more, get better educated about finances, and focus on how they could be better and do better.

Yes, the struggle is real. At the same time, the commitment to improve your quality of life and standard of living is strictly up to you. A one size fits all strategy that everyone can implement does not exist. Financial security is subjective. The amount of money you will need to feel stable is predicated upon your life conditions and overall standards. You must decide what you desire and what are you willing to do to get what you desire. While the pandemic heightened people's anxieties overall, everyday occurrences can truly cause people to spiral out of control or breathe a sigh of relief that they were committed to being better financially. So, this is how you can begin to build a solid financial future.

Dr. Nicole B. Simpson, CFP®

START WHERE YOU ARE STANDING

Now that you have acknowledged your struggles and are committed to breaking the cycle of poverty, the next step is to begin the hard work of building a firm financial foundation. Many people are lost and question how they get started. As a planner, I will always suggest you should sit down with an expert who has studied comprehensive financial planning. However, the reality is that many people are ashamed or embarrassed to bare their financial souls to anyone. They feel that they are failures or should have more. So, while that is my recommendation, let's take this journey with baby steps. Start where you are standing.

What does that mean? If you are gainfully employed, you can simply begin by reviewing the benefits your current employers offer their employees. Decades ago, when someone was hired at a company, they would go through employee training. During that training session, a human resources benefits package would be distributed to all the new hires. Sometimes the trainer will take the time to explain what is in the package. However, many people get would a folder or book or lots of papers with little or no explanation about what they mean. Today it's even more impersonal. Companies direct you to a website and you must navigate through the pages independently. Either way, inside the benefits package and posted online are all the perks and benefits associated with being a part of the staff. People are most familiar with the health care package because the need for that type of insurance is high.

In 2010, President Obama signed the Affordable Care Act into law. A major stipulation of the law was the individual mandate that required every individual to have some type of health coverage. If you chose not to secure the insurance, you would be assessed a penalty when you filed your income taxes. In 2017, after a legal challenge by the GOP led Congress, the penalty was eliminated, although the individual mandate was deemed constitutional in 2012. The Tax Cuts and Jobs Act signed into law by then President Donald J. Trump canceled the penalty effective January 1, 2019. Since Obama initially signed the Affordable Care Act into law, most employed people became familiar with the need for that benefit as soon as they filed their first income tax form.

So, people naturally fill out the paperwork or if they are married and are covered by their spouse, they will be prompted to check with their human resources representative to determine if they must sign up for their company plan or if they can decide as a family, which plan meets the needs of the family more efficiently. In the case of a married couple, it makes sense to review both plans and the company policies for each before making a health care decision which can be adjusted annually during the open enrollment period. People can change their healthcare providers under the special enrollment period if there is a qualifying life event. Several examples are based on job loss, turning age 26 and being removed from your parent's plan, marriage and/or divorce, and the addition of a baby or death in the family. If you are married with children, both spouses do not need to carry coverage so allocate the savings toward something else. After you calculate the maximum coverage for the minimum output, move forward and review additional company perks.

Many employers extend group life insurance options to their employees as a company perk. They may offer insurance that is calculated based on the employee's salary. This benefit can be employer-sponsored and/or subsidized. This basic group life insurance benefit is available and can be secured through payroll deductions. It is important to read the type of insurance that is being offered. The objective is to start where you are standing.

The benefit that will help individuals begin to accumulate wealth is through participation in the company retirement plan. The plans can vary based on the company structure. For example, most major corporations/for-profit entities offer a 401k plan. If you work for a hospital or school district, you may be familiar with a defined contribution plan like a 403B because it is associated with being a nonprofit entity typically. Federal government employees have access to a three-tiered retirement plan that includes social security, a basic benefits plan along with a thrift savings plan. Small business owners and entrepreneurs can establish plans that work best for their business models and those plans may include SEP and SIMPLE IRA plans.

The options are too numerous to count, and they have various benefits associated with the plan. What is most critical to know is that each plan offers the employee an opportunity to save for retirement. As an employee, you can have the money withdrawn from your paycheck pre-taxed and the savings can be invested. Because the employer establishes the plan, advisors are generally available to answer questions and offer guidance. Since the option is through your employer, the costs are factored into the plan design and not typically levied on the employee.

In addition to your savings, many companies will offer a company match. If you set aside a specific percentage, that varies from company to company, that company will match you anywhere from dollar to dollar or .50 cents to every dollar you set aside up to a certain percentage. Other companies offer profit sharing and still others offer a pension. In that benefits package lie the details of what is available to you. There are several conditions. The first is that you cannot withdraw the money until you reach age 59 ½ without penalty. Some exemptions are outlined that include withdrawals for qualified education expenses, the first-time purchase of a home, death, or permanent disability. Another condition is that any money the employer sets aside may be recaptured if you do not stay with the company for the set time listed in the benefits package.

For example, a major company can match your retirement savings dollar for dollar up to 5% of your income when you set aside 5%. To receive 100% of the money the company sets aside, you must be gainfully employed with them for 5 years. They will stipulate if they have included a vesting schedule. So, an employee may receive 20% of the money set aside annually until they have hit their 5th anniversary. In keeping with the example stated, if the employee chose to leave the company in year 3, they would be entitled to 60% of what the employer set aside.

Investing in the company-sponsored retirement plan makes sense for anyone committed to being financially free. There are additional incentives as well. For every dollar a person sets aside, their present taxable income is reduced accordingly for tax filing purposes. So, if someone earns $65,000 annually and they have decided to save 10% of their current income, they have set aside $6,500. That money is then deducted from their annual salary when reported to the IRS for tax calculations. The money that is set aside will not be taxed until it is withdrawn years, oftentimes, decades later. The employee has the benefit of the money being invested and taxes being deferred. Between the power of compounded interest, consistent contributions into the fund, and years before withdrawal, the earlier someone begins to save, the more opportunity they must build a solid financial future.

Today companies offer a ROTH savings option and while the funds cannot be withdrawn prematurely, the tax consequences are starkly different. A ROTH IRA or 401K is established with after-tax dollars. While the current year deduction isn't available, any money set aside for retirement grows tax-free and penalty-free. The money can be withdrawn without penalty at the age of 59 ½ and after the account has been established for 5 years. Since there are professionals who manage the company plan, regardless of the type, getting the advice of a financial advisor will help you decide how to implement your personal savings plan, and which vehicles make the most sense for you.

Health insurance, life insurance, and retirement savings are some basic benefits offered by major companies. However, companies can offer so many other incentives like adoption support, tuition reimbursement, childcare benefits, company stock options, Family Medical Leave, mental and wellness programs, disability and long-term care benefits. So, when the goal is to start the process of breaking free from financial trauma, looking at what is available to you is the perfect way to start the journey. What is extremely helpful is the fact that most benefits are payroll deducted. Once you make the emotional adjustment that your net payout from your check will be lowered per the choices you make, you will have the freedom of not worrying about anything being funded. If you remain gainfully employed, you will have the coverage you selected.

It is important to acknowledge that if someone is an entrepreneur or a small business, getting started requires more discipline and intentionality. There is beauty in being one's boss. At the same time, the responsibility of establishing a benefits package is up to the employer. An entrepreneur could secure benefits within their company from industry standard to fringe benefits. Always keep in mind that major corporations got their start as small companies and expanded over time. An independent contractor can purchase key man life insurance or set up a SIMPLE IRA or SOLO 401K. They can purchase group health insurance provided there is one additional employee besides the owner. So, while you may be challenged with having to create the benefits infrastructure, you have the flexibility to add benefits as your revenue increases. Everything does not have to be established at once.

The one thing an entrepreneur should do immediately is to review the tax benefits associated with being a business owner. I believe one of the greatest secrets in America relating to finances is how friendly the tax laws are to people who take the risk of becoming an entrepreneur. If properly understood, then one would focus on creating a benefits package sooner than later. Allow me to briefly expound on the benefits of being an entrepreneur.

The tax laws designed in the United States have always been favorable to small business owners. One of the greatest incentives is that the interpretation of the tax code has been extremely generous. The primary lens through which a business is viewed is the notion that if the expense in your line of work is "reasonable and customary in your ordinary course of business" then it can qualify as a tax deduction. So let me start at the beginning and connect it to the goal of overcoming financial trauma.

First, when you are in control of your financial future, you can rely upon your efforts to control your financial destiny. This does not take away from the reality that being your boss is extremely challenging and time-consuming. It is also very rewarding. The uncertainty in the workforce during times of recession can add a measure of insecurity that is incalculable. However, one way to combat that is to work on your business while staying in the workforce which offers you stability and a financial foundation. I try to generally encourage people to focus on both securing a W2 income and a 1099 income until they are confident enough to branch out independently. In addition, the reality of a consistent paycheck and benefits associated with working for someone instead of being the boss provides a sense of security. A major benefit is associated with health care costs. While the Affordable Care Act provides options today, before its enactment, the rising cost of healthcare made it extremely difficult to have coverage. That is a risk that I never encourage people to take. But let's say you have a great idea, you've worked on a solid business plan, and you're ready to branch out and become your boss. What should you do?

Establishing a home-based business is an ideal first step. Is it the right step for every business? I'm pretty sure one can justify why it may not make sense for a specific industry. However, it works for many, if not most. Running the business out of the home is an excellent starting point if you have the space to allocate for the business use exclusively. If the space is being used exclusively, the portion of that space can be reported as a tax deduction. For example, if you have a home that is approximately 900 square feet. The home has a finished basement that runs the span of the house, and you decided to turn the basement into your home office. Let's say that portion of the house is 30% of the total space. You can deduct 30% of the mortgage as a rental expense for the business along with the costs associated with your industry. The best way to calculate what is deductible would be to sit with a tax expert. However, if you consider what is reasonable and customary in your ordinary course of business, it will help guide you.

There are two benefits to establishing a home-based business. The first is that I fundamentally believe everyone has a gift, a skill, or a talent that is the key to their financial freedom. I also recognize many people do not explore themselves or look internally to determine what are they good at and their overall purpose in this world. However, it could potentially meet two objectives. The first is that you can find joy in working on something that brings you happiness or something you are naturally good at. It helps bolster self-confidence and to do something that comes easily while collecting a paycheck is a win-win. Anytime someone is channeling their efforts in a positive direction, it serves as a tool to offset the trauma and unease you have been accustomed to enduring. The best way to overcome any trauma is to first acknowledge it exists so that you can accept what has transpired. Your emotions need validation.

However, to connect the establishment of a business as a resolution to confront trauma needs further unpacking. Overcoming trauma takes work and a great way to process one's distress is to focus on something they are good at or enjoy doing. My traumatic experience of September 11th caused me to connect with family and friends to establish a nonprofit organization that was committed to helping people when they faced catastrophic events that left their families vulnerable. Why? When I needed help the most, the organizations that were raising money for World Trade Center survivors stripped me of my dignity when I was seeking support, causing my devastation to worsen. Channeling that despair into doing something positive and productive was my saving grace.

In the area of finances, when you are devastated by your economic position, investing in yourself helps you to rely upon your internal strength and resilience to overcome those emotions and the trauma experienced. Setting realistic goals and enlisting the support of family and friends is a great starting point. Grant Cardone said, "Your greatness is limited only by the investments you make in yourself." The only way to defeat the impact of financial trauma is by doing the work to overcome the loss. It will take hard work, and you may feel inadequate. However, this is where seeking professional support is critical. Working with a team will help guide you in the right direction.

Back to the home-based business. The second benefit is that even if the business does not turn a profit in the beginning stages, it still helps you financially. In addition to the tax deductions that are associated with the business, each year the business shows a loss, the loss is deducted from earnings from your job where you are getting a W2. Why does that matter? Well, when you are working for a company, taxes are automatically withdrawn from your paycheck based on a graduated tax scale. The best way to explain it is through an example.

Let's say you are earning $75,000 annually. Your company is going to withhold taxes for a single person with no dependents. You can report that you are married and if you have children. If you do that, the calculation for your tax deduction is already determined. At the end of the year, you will receive that W2 to file your income taxes. It will reflect how much federal, and state taxes were withheld. Without going too deep, after you input all the data for your family household, you can report the expenses from your home-based business. For a standard return, the additional form necessary for entrepreneurs is a Schedule C. When you input that data into the system, your losses will reduce your taxable income. Simply put, it serves as a benefit because the taxes you had withdrawn are most likely higher than what you will owe. Therefore, you may be entitled to a refund that can be used to help you overcome any financial pitfalls. The best way to maximize fully is to sit with professionals to appropriately establish your business and file your taxes in compliance with the IRS.

ESTABLISH NECESSARY BOUNDARIES

It is interesting to hear the myriad of responses one gets when you ask someone what they want or desire. During my multiple seasons of life transitions, I was always able to start by defining what I did not want. It made me explore that notion with greater intentionality. It's simple. Once you can clear out what you know is not most optimal for you, now you can build upon what is important, even before you identify how to prioritize. It can look something like this. I lived in the projects my entire life. I know I don't ever want to return there, and I do not want my children to experience anything associated with project life. I know I don't want to send my children to a school that is not teaching my children things necessary for their survival in this world. I know I don't want them to be exposed to depravity and uncontrollable disruption. Beginning with what you don't want creates the outline of what you envision for yourself. Even at this stage, you can begin to connect how much money you need to work with.

To construct that life plan, let's stick with what you want from a housing perspective. You can now research where you would like to reside. It's a simple search. Pick a block, a community, a town, or a school district, and begin to work on your financial outline. As you include school districts or other minimal standards, review the cost of living in that area. Where are you standing and what do you need to do to shift if necessary? That is step one. Now, you add what you do want. This requires thought and consideration. You can say, I know I want my children to be exposed to financial literacy and entrepreneurship while in school. I want the school to focus on civics and social science. I am constructing what I desire.

Understand construction takes considerable time when laying the foundation. Stop and think about your neighborhood for a moment. Reflect upon the changes within that community over time, especially if you have been at one location for many years. Think about the reliable business that has been a staple that is now going out of business or being torn down. You see the signs saying a new condo or luxury rental community is being built. It feels like nothing is visible and then suddenly, houses are appearing so rapidly that it is incomprehensible. Laying the foundation is paramount and it requires attention to detail and a great effort. It is not glamorous, and it may not be visible to the naked eye. However, when it is solidly constructed, and the foundation is sure, you will see the shell begin to develop above ground, visible and the progress can be seen by all. After the house is built, you can customize it to your preference with amenities consistent with your budget. At some point, you must stop thinking about what you don't want and don't have and focus on what you do want and do have. Just as you are declaring what you want with a new housing construction, you are the architect of your financial narrative.

This work must be done before you can realistically establish the necessary boundaries to preserve what you are committed to building. At this juncture, we have identified how emotions play a critical role in making financial decisions. The most effective tool that can override irrational spending behavior is when you have a greater desire to attain it. In other words, if your vision for your life is exactly how you mapped it out in your mind and you can see that financially you can have it, then you have a shot at showing the necessary restraint to achieve the goal.

The first thing one must do is communicate effectively what you are seeking to achieve. This is the perfect time to complete a comprehensive financial plan that allows you to answer questions relating to what you want, what that looks like, and what it will take to obtain it. It also responds to the by-when date. It's easy to say I want to retire by the age of 67 when you are 54. A great financial plan will identify what you are working with and determine if your goal is realistic. Additionally, you will have to acknowledge how your history has landed you where you are financially. Taking out retirement savings throughout the years impacted you negatively in the year of withdrawal and now if you realize you have accumulated very little. Stating your desires and measuring what you must work with to achieve those goals will guide you.

The communication needs to be concrete, and it must resonate with you first. See, you must outline what's in your heart, stay true to it, and continually set reminders to keep you focused. Once you are committed to achieving what you desire and deserve, it becomes easier to have difficult, yet necessary conversations with others. It becomes easier to say to family that you don't have the resources to help them. Here's where it gets emotionally tricky. You feel like you owe others an explanation about what you need to do with your money. I know it sounds silly when I put it like that right? However, that is exactly what you are struggling with. How do I tell my family no or that I can't? It gets easier over time when you recognize it's you or them. If you don't adjust now, you will be destined for a life of poverty the older you get.

There will be individuals, who at their advanced age, will come to terms with the reality that they are not equipped to survive financially as senior citizens. Life is complicated because you will be forced to work long past the normal retirement age. Why? You did not make the necessary shift when presented with the opportunity to get your financial affairs in order. We see it all the time. Take a trip to your local large box store and look around at the employees. At the front door are the greeters or seniors on the cash register ringing up your items. Perhaps they are walking the floor and there are a few who have something in common. They are in their mid-late 70s working a job that is generally designed for teenagers and young adults. Do you think they are there because they are looking for something to occupy their time? Or is the most likely reason that they must work, is because they rely upon that paycheck for survival? In the best-case scenario, they may have a home that is paid in full, so they are not concerned about residency. However, they have not accumulated enough assets to live off dividends and interests or an annual withdrawal from their IRA or retirement vehicles. The best-case scenario is they have social security and maybe a small pension.

If you do not convey your truth to others, it will devastate you, and you will struggle to survive from month to month. Perhaps you can avoid it by moving in with one of your children or allowing them to reside with you as a win-win situation. They can assist with the monthly expenses and help you out tremendously. Again, optimistically speaking, it can only work if you have a decent relationship with your children. Not all families grew up in the most ideal of circumstances. If your lifestyle was developed based on your trauma response, what financial lessons did you pass on to your sons and/or daughters? If we look past financial lessons, are you bonded together healthily? Where you stand now reflects that its apparent financial lack or mismanagement has been an ongoing issue. Another reality is that while your children can reside with you, they can also be the cause of your financial woes.

Guilt is a funny emotion. Oftentimes, it is when someone feels responsible or regretful for what is deemed a perceived offense. It can be real or imaginary. Parenting does not come with an instruction manual. No blueprint checks all the boxes to become the perfect role model for your children. In addition, the timing isn't always optimal. As previously stated, I was a teenage mom with only a high school diploma when my son was born. I had to drop out of college and begin work full-time. I received my first raise of 0.50 cents after working at the Military Ocean Terminal for a year and realized immediately that I needed to do something drastic before becoming a statistic. It took me months to build a blueprint of where I wanted to go financially. With the strategic plan, I avoided many pitfalls others did not. But it didn't make me the perfect mother. There were major sacrifices I had to make that took me away from my family after September 11th.

If I could rewrite history, my approach would have been different. The reason why communication is critical is that the guilt of my childhood caused me to respond in ways to protect them from anything that said we were lacking financially. I am not alone. Today I believe the best course of action is to be transparent spiritually, emotionally, physically, and economically. When your children have a clear idea about your financial status, their foundation is more secure. They have the potential to be more considerate of their requests, they may find themselves being more prudent in their spending and they may even desire to find gainful employment as their wants increase with age. My children felt the full brunt of the emotional and physical effects of September 11th, but I protected them from the financial struggles I endured. I was attempting to recover without denying them anything they desired, even when it was not feasible.

My circumstances are traditionally not normal and here's why. I have expertise in the field of investments and comprehensive planning. I also endured significant trauma in my youth. I was intentional about protecting my children while struggling to manage my fear. The insecurity was not that I would not be able to keep a roof over their heads or food on the table. I wanted to make sure if they wanted to play sports or join the drama club, they could. My focus was on discretionary expenditures, categorizing them as nondiscretionary because I did not want to disappoint them. I'm sharing this with the hope that you can see the parallel between your childhood insecurities and the choices you made and are still making today. Your response is most likely a more traditional trauma response.

What is more typical is a parent's exposure and sometimes the involuntary participation of their children in the money roller coaster ride. This can cause great friction within the family. To survive, some parents have abused their children's credit before a child can branch out into the world as a young adult. The only way for a child to rectify the damage is to press criminal charges against mom or dad. Most of the time, the child will not take that drastic measure, causing them to be financially disadvantaged just as they are starting to build a financial foundation. Another reason is based on the premise that when people are financially disadvantaged or stressed, they lash out against their loved ones. The victims of a financially caged person are often the children. The distressing, and unspoken reality is that low socio-economically status parents are more inclined to a higher risk of child abuse when they are stressed.

The connectivity to communication is predicated upon a parent needing that same child as they age if they have not gained control of their financial status. Living in poverty as a senior without the basic support of your children or family heightens the anxiety at a time when most options have been exhausted or no longer exist. If you allow the guilt of your past to dictate your future and you don't have the most ideal relationship with your children, sacrificing yourself financially will not turn things around. It will hurt you in the long run. Children who have grown up in dysfunctional families repeat the cycle and harbor resentment towards their parents. This is what financial trauma looks like in reality.

One of the most difficult conversations I dread having is to express to a mother or father that if they live long enough, they will need their children. How they treat their babies will contribute to the quality of care they will receive as they age. It isn't always a perfect metric, but if you were not there for your children, or if you were abusive, or if you didn't treat them well, you may need to find alternative solutions for growing old. The children's protective stance may require they remain at a distance from their parents for their peace of mind or security. The children can fall into the trap of financial struggles, or they can chart a financial pathway that is the total opposite of their lived experience. I chose the latter, using my childhood experience as a motivator of what not to do.

Establishing boundaries is more acceptable today than it has been in the past. You get to determine what is and is not acceptable, especially as it relates to money. It can be extremely overwhelming for you to say no. So, how can you approach it with sensitivity? One of the best ways is during your interaction with others, to indicate your unwillingness to help them at the risk of harming yourself. This requires honesty and discipline. It also provides an off-ramp of you being the first option for others in the future. When it's a close relative asking, sometimes people will lend money they cannot afford to lose. That is a boundary you should never cross again moving forward. If you cannot afford to lose it, you need to say no. You can always honestly say you do not have it to give...because you don't. This becomes even more critical the older you get because time is working against you.

Always negotiate what they are requesting unless they are willing to allow you to pay an expense directly. Someone will say they need help with a bill or groceries or to get back and forth to work. They will request a specific amount. Instead of giving them the money directly, you can offer to take them shopping, pay the bill, or provide a gas card. Why? Consider the fact that people will ask others for what they need while spending their money on the things they want. If you clearly express you are unwilling to give money away, that may dissuade them from soliciting you in the future. It will also allow you to determine if something is worthy of taking the risk of lending the money. You should never feel forced to give your money to someone else's cause. There are individuals legitimately struggling and needing help. You can encourage them to see a financial advisor to help them improve their money management. They may need to get a new job or advance their learning to become more marketable. The point is that it's up to you to help them weigh alternative options moving forward.

The final statement I will share to establish boundaries is to only give what you can without personal discomfort or resentment. The notion that someone else needs your money more than you do sounds a bit silly, doesn't it? In the age of social media, resentment is easily triggered. If you lend someone money and you are stalking their page to monitor their every move, it isn't healthy behavior. You are calculating their spending and if they do something you don't approve of your emotions go awry. This is why you must be comfortable with the reason why you are willing to help. I support a marginalized population of men and women who are formerly incarcerated. When they return home, they struggle to gain their footing financially. Many have very limited resources coupled with some habits that I frown upon.

Simply put, I am always willing to purchase groceries or clothes for an interview. I will help secure housing and essential items. I despise smoking, think it's bad for your health, and am unwilling to finance a deadly habit. It took me some time to stand on my truth financially because I knew their struggles were real. However, the comfort of others cannot be paid for by the discomfort of oneself. You will build resentment and then possibly treat others in a manner that is not the most excellent. It is also why you should never lend what you cannot afford to give.

Dr. Nicole B. Simpson, CFP®

LET GO OF THE PAST

Earlier in the book, I outlined the financial trauma that the United States of America has endured collectively. It can be difficult to overcome such great obstacles, especially if you are already fiscally vulnerable. How does one change the trajectory of their financial lives when the odds are stacked against them? We must recognize change is not easy, but it is possible. Resilience in the darkest moments of life will usher you out of the direst of situations.

With everything that occurred as a country, you cannot fully comprehend the level of trauma without looking at things that impact you personally. Job loss, unexpected illness, and death are three identifiers for most people. Natural and personal disasters such as a house fire or water damage are also devastating. When something catastrophic happens, how does one pick up the pieces and work on recovering? It can be extremely difficult to accept something that has negatively impacted your life plan. When this has occurred, it has the potential to cause serious stagnation and lack of movement. Lack of movement hinders your ability to go forward or put the pieces of your life back together again.

Some people think a person declaring you must move forward is insensitive or they do not understand what you are going through or how you feel. While there are individuals who do not express empathy when delivering sage advice, you must begin to accept that you cannot change anything that happened in your past. Moving forward is essential for your overall well-being. In the area of finances, we often regret some of the choices we have made, particularly when times are rough. This is when you must adopt a disciplined approach to build something substantive. I find it fascinating how people convince themselves they are ready, but will not seek the guidance of a coach, mentor, expert, or even an accountability partner. If you were able to break bad financial habits, why did you wait until your condition was so traumatic? Something did not connect with what you said you wanted and what you were doing.

In the previous chapter, I talked about protecting my children from some of the disappointments I experienced. Trying to make up for what happened in your past will cause you to jeopardize future opportunities. My saving grace was my commitment to systematic investments. From the time I started working, I set aside money and outlined it in my budget as an expense, a reoccurring, non-negotiable bill. I had ten years of systematically investing before the tragedy of September 11th. I fell into the category of children who grew up and decided they would do the opposite of what they saw their parents do. And it worked until I realized that I failed to consider how my emotional decisions were negatively impacting my overall savings. Think about it. Have you ever placed something in your pockets thinking everything was secure only to find out you had a hole all along? Consistently saving and investing while spending money frivolously is counterproductive. We justify our behavior because it's our children or we deserve it, or we love someone we may be trying to impress.

Eventually, I had to accept the reality that my behavior was unsustainable. Something had to change. You must learn how to say no to others if you are serious about seizing the opportunity to course correct. Sometimes it means downsizing or going on a financial fast. You may be familiar with intermittent fasting. It is a strategic plan to help someone manage their weight and possibly reverse several diseases.

Some people who are spiritual use it as an exercise to draw closer to God. The person minimizes their food intake and sometimes abstains altogether for a set period. A financial fast is very similar. A person decides they are setting up certain parameters for spending. Whenever you get the urge to purchase something that is not a necessity, you are committed to exercising discipline, and you choose to abstain. If you are starting where you stand, setting up a savings strategy systematically is the next critical step. However, you must also plug up the holes and that is difficult to do. You owe it to yourself to prepare for the unknown and inevitable events in life. I may be biased, but I am convinced that children find reasons to have issues with their parents. I think it's a part of the "I'm a teenager" phase of their lives. My experience is that they snap out of it after a while.

When you stop competing with your past, your future looks brighter. Sorrow cannot be avoided, and you cannot make up for anything that occurred. It can make you feel powerless and out of control. Yet, there is hope. You can take control of your circumstances and steer your life ship in the direction you desire. Being realistic and setting measurable goals that you are willing to write down is critical. Confront what happened head-on and decide this time you will gain the upper hand because you don't want to stay in the place of lack any longer. You have overstayed your welcome. It's time to move forward.

COMMIT TO STAYING POSITIVE

Sometimes you must be extremely careful to strike a balance between being practical and too optimistic. Negativity and despair have led your actions and responses long enough so being excited about this new journey makes sense. I want to caution you to be honest and pragmatic. Your circumstances may not change rapidly, but your mindset must. Keep in mind you are starting where you stand. Recently, I completed a continuing education course on the continuous rise of long-term care expenses. What struck me as a planner was the position of industry insiders based on current laws and the lack of resources the government is willing to provide for aging men and women. It is important solely because it has taken some time for you to get a great financial footing. Any information that can be perceived to be overwhelming can hinder progress.

Nevertheless, it is a reality that must be confronted while you are gaining financial ground. The consensus is that if you have between $50,000 and one million dollars, you need to plan for your long-term care needs. The number was so low, in my opinion, that I can see others viewing the challenges associated with aging as an obstacle. Throughout the book, we have identified multiple steps to implement so that you can begin a healthy journey toward financial stability. It is possible to save the minimum suggested amount in your job's savings vehicle. Without calculating a company match or any earnings potential, saving $200 per month for twenty years will help you achieve your goal. Hopefully, those two examples place things into proper perspective.

Earlier, when dealing with how to get started, I used the example of someone who earned $65,000 annually. If they were to allocate 10% towards retirement, without the company match and without considering investment growth, the twenty-year projection ceases to exist because you will hit a savings of $50,000 in approximately eight years. However, if you add the company match and a simple savings projection, the goal of saving that amount can be achieved years earlier. This is why staying positive matters. Getting started can oftentimes be the greatest challenge.

I adopted a practice in 2007 when I established my firm with very few assets under management. I built my business by encouraging people to systematically invest, save in their retirement accounts, and protect their families with permanent life insurance with a long-term care rider. My goal was to get people to commit to saving at least $350-$400 each month. I recognized that based on my target market, I needed to build an infrastructure that would help me remain in business while I educated and encouraged people in my community that wealth accumulation was possible. I also needed to show them it made sense and that I did not simply give advice, I implemented those suggestions and strategies in my life. As I stated earlier, before September 11th, 2001, I had ten years of evidence that saving a small dollar amount each month would serve to be beneficial over time.

I revealed my medical challenges. I was also battling with physical complications that forced me into private practice initially. The diagnosis of asthma, COPD, anxiety, and depression was not a part of my life plan. I had to shift. I was medically classified as permanently, and partially disabled. My goal was simple. I needed to earn a full-time income on a part-time basis. The main objective was to help historically marginalized and oppressed communities know there was a way out of financial lack. It would be slow and steady. It would be difficult at times, but it would be a life changer if they were willing to do the work and give themselves some time to build. I also needed time to prove I could overcome financial trauma with a strategic plan, a commitment to savings, and a true understanding of how to consider if my emotional responses to life circumstances had financial consequences.

The first few years were challenging. With the business being established during a recession, people were initially afraid to commit to anything. Simultaneously, I was able to better comprehend why people shy away from professional advice. It is because they feel inadequate or embarrassed that they have not accumulated much or in some cases anything at all. However, the net worth of Americans in 2022 according to the Federal Reserve was a mere $192,700.

While it jumped significantly even after COVID-19, it isn't a true measurement. Think about it. The more highly compensated positions are often found on the east and west coasts and the savings tend to be much higher. However, you must recognize that the Federal Reserve is conducting a national average, which includes low-income-producing states as well. Therefore, the averaging formula for all Americans is fundamentally flawed. Statistics show that the top 5% of the wealthiest Americans have a net worth of just over $1 million. But hitting $1 million isn't impossible. The question is, do you have enough time on your hands and are you committed to accumulating wealth? There is always a pathway to saving 1 million dollars, even if you work hard and you don't have a glamorous high-paying job. Time matters.

While it is possible, it may not be feasible based on when you have your aha moment. If you haven't been committed to accumulating wealth until your mid-forties, you have lost precious time. Thomas Corley, the author of *Rich Habits* compiled data that suggested it takes the average self-made millionaire 32 years to achieve their goal. So, if you start saving in your retirement plan with your $65,000 income when you were in your early to mid-20s, and you set aside an additional $3000-$3500 annually with after-tax dollars, if you were properly invested and you never withdrew anything, you will accumulate a net worth of over 1 million dollars sometime between age 50 and 60. If you purchase a home, establish a business, and steadily increase your savings over the years, you will achieve your goals sooner.

When you begin to examine the numbers, it becomes less intimidating. Going back to the strategy I crafted when I became an entrepreneur in 2007, I was able to encourage middle-class working employees that they could acquire a net worth of more than 1 million dollars. While life continues to happen, many are first-generation wealth accumulators. In addition, if a person did not accumulate 1 million dollars, they left a substantial inheritance to the next generation, positioning them to achieve such a lofty goal. It isn't about saving a stated amount of money. It is about living comfortably for your entire life understanding that the decisions you make earlier in your working years will determine what you can do as you age.

Going back to the rising costs of long-term care, and the recommendation that people address health care costs, you cannot remain complacent. If you have accumulated at least $50,000 and you are committed to breaking free from financial trauma, accumulating that amount becomes easier. Because you have decided to focus on your financial well-being, planning is more complex. In addition to wealth accumulation, you cannot ignore the need to protect your assets. It makes things more complicated, but it is possible. Always remember that time is your friend. The moment you begin to shift, you are positioning yourself to protect yourself and what you have the time to accumulate.

Thinking you can simply focus on wealth accumulation is being too optimistic. As your net worth increases, you can be easily lulled into the misconception that nothing will happen to disrupt your objectives. I didn't think September 11th was ever possible. The people who have endured a fire never thought it could happen to them and when someone is diagnosed with a chronic illness, they can't believe the doctor. Life happens and there are uncontrollable variables that have a detrimental impact. When a catastrophic event occurs, one must deal with the incident at hand. Almost immediately thereafter, the question about finances rears its ugly head. How will this tragedy impact me economically?

If you are truly committed to building assets, you must remain positive so that you have the tenacity to stay the course. Getting upset and regressing into old habits is taking the easy route. Placing things in their proper perspective while remaining committed to building is the best course of action. So, how can you quiet the noise in your head that is telling you what you are looking to accomplish is fruitless? Set several goals that can be celebrated as you hit those thresholds. For example, when I begin to work with someone and they have never saved any money, I would share with them that we would celebrate when they saved their first $1000. Why? Gobankingrates.com completed a survey in November 2023 inquiring about how much money Americans have for emergencies. The statistics indicated that nearly half of Americans have less than $500 to cover an emergency or an unexpected expense. Therefore, having $1000 in savings is a huge deal.

Don't settle for one successful goal. I celebrate when someone hits $5000, $10,000, $25,000, $50,000, and $100,000 as well. The constant reiteration that you are moving in the right direction encourages you to remain positive.

EMBRACE YOUR NEW NORMAL

Adopting a new lifestyle takes discipline and commitment. There is an old saying that says the best way to eat an elephant is to take one bite at a time. To tackle your financial future requires a disciplined approach. Making drastic shifts that require a sacrifice of your behavior or spending habits may prove to be inefficient over time. The disciplined approach will be your guide. It requires a transformation of your mind and constant reiteration that the adjustments you are making will prove to be beneficial eventually. Let me break it down further. One major struggle people collectively understand is the commitment to remain healthy. It may require working out, changing your dietary habits, and avoiding stressful situations or environments, to name a few.

People who attempt to diet find they can experience initial success. Yet after a while, any weight loss fades away the moment they discontinue the steps they originally initiated. It is the same with implementing a savings strategy. You will stumble. It happens. It takes time for the discipline to be in full effect. What will have a significant impact on your success is how you define emergency. Most financial plans suggest you set aside 3-6 months of emergency cash. You calculate that number based on your monthly nonexpendable expenditures. That includes, but is not limited to, rent, gas and electric, groceries, auto expenses, etc. What you have just identified is what it will cost you to maintain your standard of living during lean times. I recommend you measure how much your vocational and family dynamics. These are general principles, not specific to any specific situation.

Several career paths have proven to be almost recession-proof. Layoffs aren't as impactful in education, first responders, or social services. So, if you are in fields that typically have job security, that is a major consideration. If you live in a two-income household and one income has job security, you can work towards the three months because the anticipation is that one wage earner will provide stability or a floor of income. That salary can be used to provide the entire family with a sound financial floor. If you are a single-earning household, you want to build your emergency cash closer to the six months of nonexpendable expenses to give yourself time to adjust your financial plan. If you have two incomes in the household, yet one is vulnerable and potentially higher, you want to set aside six months as well. For example, for people in sales, those who work on commissions, or entrepreneurs, your income may not be steady. Your weekly earnings fluctuate based on a variable such as hours worked, products sold, or services rendered. You have variables that can impact your income, so you want to protect your standard of living as well.

I want to include an additional consideration to the need for setting aside 3-6 months of emergency cash and how we define it. It is usually income, dependents, and debt that are the primary factors. However, think about when you have experienced an emergency in the past. Outside of being released from your job, what were other examples that caused you financial stress? Did your car need repairs? Did something in the house stop working? Did a dependent fall ill and disrupt your income? Did someone in your extended family die unexpectedly and you had to travel or help absorb the financial costs? Did someone else have an emergency that impacted you financially? I know that you have been conditioned to think about non-discretionary expenses as the calculus for emergency savings, but I want you to expand that list by considering at least one to two of the additional costs that are realistic emergencies.

You can build your net worth by considering your short-term, intermediate-term, and long-term goals at the same time. If you do not make the adjustments in your life as a stressful exercise and you classify your savings appropriately, you can take the financial hit an emergency brings over time without losing significant ground. It takes time to build, and you must clearly define an emergency for the strategy to work effectively. Needing a break or you deserve to treat yourself after all you have endured are not the most excellent reasons to squander what you are attempting to build. If you breach your agenda and then your car breaks down at the most inopportune time, you will be more emotionally and economically devastated trying to manage.

Saving on your job for retirement is always the long-term savings bucket. It is pre-taxed and you cannot withdraw any funds without penalty until you turn 59 ½. While companies may offer you the option to take a loan out against it, I strongly advise against it. It will impact you at retirement. There are moments where it may become necessary such as when you need to pay for college for a child or you are looking to purchase a new home. Those are exceptions and one should still look elsewhere if possible. The next bucket depends on how much you have decided to set aside for your new normal. Even if you are starting with $50 each pay period, it's a step in the right direction. There are mutual fund companies and online investment companies that will allow you to invest small amounts to accumulate fractional shares of stocks, bonds, and mutual funds. I believe your emergency cash accumulation should be inconvenient for you to withdraw. I find that we define emergencies differently if they require us to do significant work. It's that mindset adjustment I continue to mention. Now, back to the commitment of $50. You may want to split the money between liquid assets and investments. That covers your short-term and intermediate-term goals. You can increase the amount of savings incrementally. I like to meet with my clients annually and the goal is to encourage them to increase their savings each year. You may find that this is where a financial planner would be most helpful. For anyone unwilling to take that leap, try your local bank because most banks offer investment advisory services. Sit with them and allow them to help you devise a strategy. They work for the bank and would love the chance to earn your business. More importantly, you are a client and it's a service they offer because you have chosen them to house your money. Call it a perk.

Since this book addresses overcoming financial trauma, when embracing your new normal, there is oftentimes an old fear or insecurity that rears its ugly head the moment you begin to see progress. I thought about dealing with it when I spoke on debt (refer to what is financial trauma), but I didn't want it to get lost in the conversation. Many people are excited about this new journey and that's great. They like to see the money grow over time and find security in knowing they have a few hundred or a few thousand dollars set aside. It is counterproductive if you are saving money while still maintaining debt, that doesn't make sense. Bad debt, like credit card debt, is comparable to the example I stated earlier where you are saving in a pocket that has holes in it. Let me break it down.

The average credit card company charges you interest to purchase items on credit. That interest rate can be as low as 0% for a set period or as high as 34%. Some people have enough discipline to pay the debt before the interest sets in. Strategically speaking, I have no objections to that. I understand the benefits that are associated with using specific cards. It can be the added insurance for the actual purchase or steep discounts and that's fine. Just be prepared to pay the bill in full each month to get the best of both worlds. However, if you maintain an outstanding balance on a credit card while saving money in an interest-bearing or money market account, you are paying a much larger amount on the debt you owe than you are receiving from the money you have accumulated. Pay off the debt!

Here's where the fear comes in. You are afraid that something will happen, and you will not have the resources to manage if you give up what you have. It's your security blanket and you are not willing to part with it just like Linus in the cartoon strip Peanuts. The character carried that blanket everywhere because it brought him comfort and he was distressed every time he had to part with it, even when it needed to be washed. If you dig deeper into the story, there were different moments when Linus had to part with his blanket, yet he always managed to retrieve it after some time. Reasons for the separation varied, however, they were all to either protect it, help someone else, or for the greater good to be determined by the specific circumstance. Paying off high-interest credit debt allows you to save more over the long term. When the debt is paid, you have more money to allocate towards savings and can be used to rebuild more rapidly.

You cannot allow fear or insecurity to disrupt your overall agenda. Because this journey is being taken in strides, not sprints, we want to adopt a holistic approach to achieve the goal of financial security. At the same time, we want to acknowledge how we feel and process those emotions methodically.

Allow me to address the elephant in the room. Much of what I am suggesting may appear to take too long. If we are being honest, delayed gratification isn't an ideal many embrace in the 21st century. Today's society desires instant gratification. Think about this, you can "cook" an entire meal in the microwave, and I admit, air fryers are one of the greatest inventions ever made. The notion that a get-rich-quick strategy for financial success is all that you need, is the very reason why people suffer unnecessary loss. Besides, if it were available and a proven strategy, most people would jump on the bandwagon right away. It is almost always the people who had a twist of luck or fate that benefit financially, while many others suffer. Look at the frenzy associated with meme stocks during the height of the pandemic.

Investopedia initiated a research report verifying that many new, inexperienced investors began trading stocks and cryptocurrency. When the market turned sharply negative initially, quite a few new investors were devastated even further. The losses were short-lived but there were some success stories. Novice investors began to advise on social media platforms regarding their profits. It became crazy with lessons on how to leverage to trade and advice on what stocks to purchase. The stock selections did not have professional advisory logic behind the recommendations. It was a polarizing time because people were home, not making money, and looking for ways to get rich. One quick note of advice; anytime someone cannot explain the investment rationale, it is best to disregard the advice.

Slow and steady may require sacrificing in the moment, but it will produce longer-term stability over time. It's delayed profitability. As a teenage mom, I could not do the things my friends did each weekend. First, I didn't have the money, and one evening out meant getting someone to care for the kids, feeding them before I walked out the door, and then needing money that would allow me to keep up with the Joneses. This affects everyone. If you're in college and everyone is hanging out or you're at the office and the coworkers are meeting at a local restaurant for happy hour and karaoke. Even in the church arena, going to a conference to feed your spirit has an exorbitant financial cost that brings temporary satisfaction or contentment.

Now, I'm not suggesting you sit home and be a money miser. I am suggesting that you plan more strategically so that you can have a balance between enjoying life today without risking the financial stability for tomorrow. However, you still need to be able to afford to do the things you desire. For years, I could not go away on vacation because my responsibilities were too great, but it was a worthwhile sacrifice. I was honest with myself, and I learned how to manage fun on a budget. Now, I'm not flexing, but since I still have the same friends from my early 20s, they can attest that today I travel where I want, whenever I want, and the cost is never a factor.

Peer pressure can be brutal. Honesty about your circumstances with those who are closest to you goes a long way. Your friends may not have to care for an aging parent, they may not have children, and they may not have the responsibilities you have. Use wisdom so you can have the best of both worlds. If you choose to join others for dinner, be clear that you require individual checks or select the "bring your own brown bag" restaurant to control the costs. Suggest a matinee movie or stay home when the girls or fellas plan a quick getaway that you didn't consider in your budget. Trust me, there will always be another party, another trip, or another show.

BUILD THE LIFE YOU DESIRE

One of the most provoking questions I ask people is designed to make them reflect upon what they desire the most. I referred to it earlier when addressing emotions versus money. It is, "If money were not an issue, what would you do with your life?" I believe the greatest medicine for a fulfilling life is to focus on including things that bring you joy and peace. In the real world of responsibilities that cannot be ignored, work is not optional. If you are willing to find a balance between what you desire and what you must do, the equilibrium will emerge. However, wishful thinking will not make those things manifest over time. It requires work. You must be willing to build the life you desire. What does that look like?

I have an exercise that I've shared over the years that has proven to yield positive results. Consider the things that make you happy and begin to envision yourself engulfed in actions that reflect your values. Go back in your memory bank to see what has endured the test of time. What comes to mind? Sit with it-allocate time to meditate on it. It may be something that showcases a skill or gift you may have. It may be something you dreamed about doing if you ever had time. It could even be something you are willing to do to support or serve other people. If you could be compensated for doing what you loved, would you pursue that elusive desire?

Let's take another step. While you are meditating on that desire, begin to write down what it looks like in your dreams. What would that business look like? What is the ideal job? Who do you want to surround yourself with? Do you see yourself creating? It's a powerful sight to see what you want on paper glaring at you. It moves it from being abstract and imaginary to something potentially tangible. Don't just write it down, take a moment to research what it will take to make it happen. I have found Google and YouTube to be the most powerful tools when figuring out how to accomplish something. There are too many tutorials for virtually everything, and we are officially out of excuses for not doing what we want to do. It takes time, effort and energy to get started.

After you research, then you can think about money. Make the connection between what you love, what has your heart, and how you can benefit from it financially. I think examples can illuminate this point more precisely. If you love to bake, then bake. When I was in business for about a decade, I met a woman who was widely recognized for making rum cakes. The requests were so overwhelming that someone suggested she consider establishing a business and that's how our paths crossed. It wasn't a simple solution called just start baking cakes and add a price to the cake. We sat down to discuss what she desired to do and how did she feel when she made a cake. After further discussions, she knew it was her passion, she was great at it, but she was unwilling to focus her energy on something so erratic. So, we created a strategic plan that allowed her to benefit both emotionally and economically.

The rum cake lady established a business while maintaining her traditional job. She used the money she earned to catch up on her savings for retirement and took advantage of having a home-based business. Simultaneously, she increased her quality of life making sure that she baked because of the joy it brought her, and not because of the money. She was content with having additional money to make her life more comfortable. Being known as the rum cake lady also gave her purpose and identity, which she embraced. Most importantly, she maintained balance so that she would not begin to resent what she had always found comfort in doing.

I can recall a man who spent more years incarcerated than he was free. After having a deep conversation, I learned that his expression of love and gratitude for people who supported him after being released from prison was to detail their cars. He was almost sixty years old with a very limited education and quite honestly, his vocabulary handicapped him as well. But he loved his community, and he loved to detail cars. It made me recall the stereotype that depicts how one can define how men treat their women by simply looking at how they treat their cars. Anyway, he was so passionate about showing his gratitude to leaders in the community, including law enforcement, that many of the officers began to request he detail their cars. Because of his age and his history of being incarcerated, he never worked long enough to secure forty quarters to qualify for social security.

Quick lesson. To qualify for social security, you must accumulate credits, limited to four credits each year which takes ten years to meet the requirements. There is an amount you must earn to have the credit count and in 2024, that amount is $1730. For this gentleman, he relied on tips the people gave him, and those tips represented his only source of revenue. The volume of requests became so great that we established an auto detailing business, and he secured a contract to detail the police cars in his local community. It was not even a consideration for him, yet the opportunity presented itself and he continues to earn a few hundred dollars each week doing what he loves most. Now, unfortunately, he is destined for a life of poverty because he has a limited timeline to accumulate resources. However, he has a strong family network that will provide him with food and shelter for the remainder of his life.

Finally, you've heard my reason why Generation X Community Association was established. My family decided to be a voice for young people in our local community in advocacy and politics. Then my 9/11 experience devastated me to the core of my existence. I needed to educate and empower the marginalized and oppressed communities about economic justice. I needed to let minorities know that financial freedom was possible for them as well, they didn't need to live beneath their standards. I wanted them to focus on placing a life plan in place before something devastating or catastrophic happened. Serving the nonprofit organization illuminated my purpose for existing. In addition, I thought about the ripple effect my commitment to education would produce. A ripple effect is an action or event that continues to produce results. After I began serving my community, I wanted to have an impact that would last beyond my lifetime.

I was invited into the prison system shortly after the tragedy of September 11th, 2001, to share my story of resilience and to encourage women on how to pick up the pieces of their lives after they have endured a catastrophic experience that devastated them physically, emotionally, and economically. During my time with the women, they asked me if I would advocate on their behalf. I was both overwhelmed and honored. Let me also say I was clueless as to what advocacy would entail. I was clear that because they asked, I would do whatever I could to stand with them. This is how I learned about the ministry of David Wilkerson.

David Wilkerson first captured my interest as I began to research how I could best serve individuals who could not advocate for themselves. My focus was to create a support system to offer returning citizens a strategic plan that would allow them to pick up the pieces of their lives spiritually, emotionally and economically. While society peers may say an incarcerated individual's challenges were self-inflicted wounds, one cannot dismiss the fact they have endured trauma. David Wilkerson had a passion for teenagers and young adults who were struggling with alcohol and drug addictions. In the late 1950s, he traveled to New York and began to minister to gang-affiliated members and drug addicts. His desire to help them led to the establishment of Teen Challenge in 1960.

Teen Challenge, which still exists today, is a network of Christian faith-based corporations whose primary objective is to offer rehabilitation services to people struggling with addiction. The organization quickly became a potential last stop before an individual was incarcerated. He dedicated his life to trying to keep the youth from being incarcerated. I desired to ensure that when a man or woman was released from prison, they would never return. We were able to establish something positive through the organization. Building the life you desire is possible, and it can serve as the reason for your willingness to shift your mindset over time. The opportunity to channel your energy doing something positive and productive can be quite liberating. Focusing on a cause that is bigger than you, can sometimes change perspectives so much that spending frivolously or recklessly feels so irresponsible that you become more conscious about how blessed you truly are.

Your motivating factor is not as important as the underlying message that you can change course and live a purposeful life as you envision. There is a saying that people use to justify unwise life and ultimately financial decisions. They would declare that you only live once so you may as well be happy. The truth is that you live every day, and you only die once.

Each day you awake, you can chart the course of your day. You can decide to stay doing what you are doing now, or you can choose to do things differently to yield different results. You could work on what's most important to you a bit each day. You could take a new bite out of that proverbial elephant to achieve your goals.

I have one final consideration for you. This is a lesson I am still learning daily, so you are never too old to embrace a teachable moment. Enjoy the journey of discovery. Getting to a certain place in life, achieving a major milestone, or accomplishing a major goal are all admirable. At the same time, not pausing to appreciate progress or celebrate the wins and obstacles you overcome along the way are missed opportunities. Many can identify with trying to recover economically, especially if they were devastated by a catastrophic loss. The impact of September 11th, 2001, had a ripple effect on my life for over a decade. It felt like every time I thought I regained financial footing, one small incident occurred that threw me off course. And I'm the expert. So, I understand the feelings of hopelessness and helplessness, especially when you are struggling to survive from day to day. The biggest distinction was that I knew I was building something I could be proud of. I knew my life had significance and purpose. When I first started on the road to recovery, I had major milestones that remained a blur in my life. I had several achievements that meant nothing economically, so I minimized their significance.

Yet, I stayed the course. I knew where I was trying to go and in January 2014, I shifted the methodology, not the plan. It was a simple adjustment that yielded a better pathway to mental wellness. The shift mentally impacted my ability to earn more. Now, I am an entrepreneur, so my earnings potential is admittedly different from someone working for a company. However, I know the results are possible for us all. I began to outline my progress, and I structured celebratory posts into my business plan. What did it do for me? As I continued to work on my dreams, I didn't originally track my progress, so I had nothing to celebrate. The moment I began to acknowledge myself, it was like a dam had broken. I was placing value on how far I had traveled.

If you are building the life you desire, you will find greater joy in the journey. Others may ask, how did you get there or how did you arrive? You will have an answer because you will know how hard you worked, the sacrifices you made, the obstacles you had to overcome, and the times you wanted to give up, but you chose to take another step toward your dreams.

Dr. DeForest B. Soaries, Jr., a most impactful mentor, instructed me to complete an exercise that was extremely transformative in my life. After encouraging me to understand who I am and reminding me statistically that being an African American woman Certified Financial Planner was a huge deal, he told me to write down fifty amazing things to describe myself. The exercise boosted my confidence and helped me to see how credible AND incredible I am.

The assurance that you are worthy of what you desire provides you with the ammunition you need to fight off anything that promotes doubt, insecurities or negative thoughts. Take a moment to write that list of fifty things that define you. Fifty things that make you proud to be you. Write that list and every time you are overwhelmed or uncertain or discouraged, you pull out that list and encourage yourself. You deserve the life you desire.

STAY THE COURSE

In July 2024, on a Wednesday morning, I entered my office to meet with an individual who was once a client. This individual had endured physical and emotional trauma that caused significant changes in their life. They were now considering retirement and wanted to connect because I had not abandoned them during very trying financial seasons in their life. Whenever they called, I treated them with the respect and dignity they deserved. While they could never re-establish a business relationship with me, they implemented every suggestion I gave, and their obedience paid off. They are set to retire with a seven-figure net worth, and they were excited to work with me again. At the end of the meeting, I turned to my assistant and uttered these simple words, "I thank God I stayed the course."

Financial trauma is real. It is devastating and it is difficult to recover from, especially if it is the result of a separate traumatic incident or experience. You may have been physically, emotionally or financially abused. You may have grown up in poverty and could not fight against your socio-economic conditions for a long time. Perhaps you lost everything or someone tragically and that is what caused you to spiral out of control financially. It's life and life happens. We cannot change the events of the past, but we have the strength and resolve to move forward, not allowing life's circumstances or conditions to defeat us.

I do not simply teach about financial trauma. I have lived the experience, and I know its impact is real. Growing up in poverty, enduring physical and sexual abuse, and being directly involved in the tragedy of September 11th, 2001, had an impact. At the same time, I knew I deserved a fruitful, life of purpose. With that, I recognized it required work and the work I was willing to do had to consider broken pieces, stressors that could not be ignored, and a true understanding of the residual memories that could potentially serve as stumbling blocks were a part of my strategic plan.

Staying the course pays dividends over time. If you remain focused on doing what you love, the money will come. After being in the securities industry since 1991, and deciding I wanted to eventually establish my practice in the late 1990s, I stood on the plan. I endured many challenges and lost everything I acquired several times in the midst, but I did not give up. The principles I adopted early were built on the framework set by George S. Clason in the book *The Richest Man in Babylon.* As a person of faith, I have always invested 10% into God, ministry work, and service. That was personal. But the book caused me to subscribe to what I live by today and that is a 10-10-80 rule. It's 10% of my earnings to God, 10% to myself, and 80% are my everyday expenditures.

Clason talks about the 10% to self. His book encourages people to pay themselves first, regardless of how little they earn. In your building stage, how you invest in yourself matters. I am hopeful you understand now the importance of setting some resources aside for retirement first. Then if you have a skill or are gifted, you are creative enough and confident in yourself to construct something with that skill or talent. It is up to you to set boundaries and develop the life you desire. You should be your biggest cheerleader and every decision you make should consider the financial repercussions over the long term. If you made small, systematic investments into yourself today, tomorrow you will benefit from the sacrifices of today.

The remaining 80% will establish your overall standard of living over time. It should guide your thinking and help you gauge areas that need attention so you can consistently improve your socio and/or economic stature if that is your desire. Everyone is not seeking to acquire millions of dollars in their lifetime. Some people have a beautiful plan that does not have a huge financial cost. They want to be happy, live healthy, and do not need anything else. Whatever the goal is, your plan must consider all variables, not merely a calculation of numbers. We must go deeper and understand how you feel, how you connect to, and how you process the notion of wealth accumulation, maintenance, and distribution.

To stay the course is to acknowledge and accept the fact that everything that has transpired to this point happened. There is nothing that can be done to change the past. We can learn from it and move forward. Every time you spent money you didn't have, every time you tapped into your savings and depleted it, when you bounced a check or didn't pay a bill, leave it all in the past. And hear me, you will probably do it again. We are working on changing, but it will not occur overnight. There is room for grace.

The next step is to understand what caused you to make the financial decisions you have made historically. What adjustments are you willing to make immediately, and which ones will take time to tackle? If you start where you are standing, you will take advantage of the benefits available on your job. You will use payroll deduction as much as possible. At a minimum, you can focus on health insurance, life insurance, and retirement savings. That is a great start, and you are on your way.

Now we want to channel our energy into upward mobility and what that looks like. This may require additional education and certification. You may need to focus on establishing and working on a business that brings you joy or just more money. You may have determined your emotional bandwidth has been stretched too thin. Counseling to help you process the experiences of your past that continue to weigh you down is necessary. Working through how you became who you are is always helpful. It is okay if you desire professional support in navigating that specific leg of the journey. Self-discovery in the process is liberating.

Do not give up. There will be times when it feels like you are racking up losses or missing the mark. It's easy to say this may not be the way for you. However, I have a heartfelt belief that one can only fail if one gives up. Everything else is a lesson on the pathway to success. You also grow amid missteps, and you pick up valuable information that will be useful on this journey of life. Nothing is squandered. Life is like a puzzle. Every piece and every experience are relevant in cultivating your life plan. Do not throw away or try to block anything believing it wasn't critical. If you have ever put a puzzle together, the worst thing is to get to the end of the puzzle and have one piece missing. Every experience matters.

Put yourself first. You cannot harbor guilt for wanting to ensure that you are financially fit. As you grow older, there will come a time when you hang up your proverbial toolbelt and stop building. It is called retirement. What you have accumulated must be sufficient to sustain you for an average expected life expectancy of 17 years if you reach age 65. When you prolong preparing for that eventual reality, you limit your options at the most inopportune time. In addition, you must consider your ability to work beyond a normal retirement age.

I recently engaged with an individual who had an entire career and retired comfortably. Then that person began to help others, splurge excessively and squandered their resources. They had to return to work full-time and now the goal is to hit ten years with the company so they can have additional benefits. That means they will not retire until after they are in their 80s. Fortunately for them, they are doing what they love, they were able to stay within their field, and they didn't want to sit home alone wasting the days away. It was a win/win. It was also a great risk and one that I do not recommend people take.

Finally, meet with someone who has experience and expertise in financial planning. It is a worthy investment. The second major takeaway from George S. Clason for me was about using wisdom when making financial decisions. He addressed the fact that advice is freely given without parameters. It is up to you to determine which advice is worthy of your consideration. Listening to family and friends who are not showing the benefits of being financially free doesn't make sense. It is the blind leading the blind. Why take advice from someone who is not implementing the very strategies they are telling you to employ? If the people are looking to borrow from you, then maybe your strategic plan is stronger.

I will leave on this note. It took me a much longer time to acquire and accumulate than I envisioned when I was that little girl in the fourth grade visiting the New York Stock Exchange. I knew one day I would own companies that had a ticker symbol flashing across television screens. I didn't consider being a financial advisor until my first vocational plan was interrupted due to my unplanned pregnancy and I needed to shift. However, if I had not implemented immediately everything I studied early in my career, I would not have been capable of withstanding all the financial storms that came my way after the tragedy of September 11th. The sooner you focus on your financial future, the more time you will have to dedicate to being financially free.

I am no different from you. I came out of the worst socio-economic environment with limited education and opportunities. I had the deficit of trauma as an accessory, and I had the determination that I would not allow my childhood experiences to chart the course of my future. I had grit and knowledge. I share this because I am a witness that where you start in the journey toward financial freedom doesn't have to dictate where you will land. However, if you do not consider how your childhood has shaped how you see money, it can become problematic when you make financial decisions that do not align with your desired goals.

Staying the course isn't always easy but it is possible. How hard are you willing to work toward living the life you desire? Let today be the day you break free from financial trauma and build the life you have always envisioned!

About Dr. Nicole B. Simpson, CFP®

Reverend Dr. Nicole B. Simpson, CFP® is a practitioner with over thirty years of experience in the securities industry which she entered in 1991 and holds Series 7, 63, and 65 Securities licenses.

On September 11, 2001, her life was drastically altered as a financial planner working at 2 World Trade Center on the 73rd floor. Simpson was still in the building on the 44th floor when Tower 2 was hit during the World Trade Center attacks. Today, Simpson compassionately assists families on how to begin to walk along the road to recovery when faced with a catastrophic, unexpected disaster. She is actively involved in spiritual, emotional, and economic empowerment.

A compelling empowerment speaker, television/radio personality, and author, Dr. Simpson travels throughout the United States teaching in a practical and easy-to-understand manner. Her simple approach motivates everyone who hears her message to take action to change their future. Her commitment is to engage people with the thought, "If money were not an issue, what would be your life's purpose?"

Dr. Nicole's took shape when she turned seven years old. Gifted with a Bible by her mother, she spent most of her time in her room reading the red words in that Bible, sparking her interest. Those red words told her to do good to please God and taught her how to pray. It was through reading the scriptures, that she learned how to seek God's comfort amidst every storm.

Like most individuals, she has suffered unexpected, significant personal tragedies that affected her entire family emotionally and financially. What is critical, but often avoided, is the experience and willingness to share strategies that instruct others about overcoming unexpected disasters that can stagnate one's personal life. "How does one pick up the pieces of their life and move toward their ordained purpose?" Not only does she answer those questions, but she also puts into perspective the necessary process and steps to recover well emotionally and financially.

In January 2016, she embarked on a new life journey becoming the Senior Pastor of Micah 7 Ministries located in Piscataway, NJ. Her media profile includes appearances on TEDx Mavili Square in May 2023, ABC News, CNN News, BBC World News, Huffington Post, Crains NY Business, Fox News, PBS and UPN 9. She is a Board Member of the CFP Board Center for Financial Planning Diversity Advisory Group, Chair of the Generation X Community Association, and Provost of the Dare 2 Dream Institute. She frequently speaks on the lecture circuit and has authored several books on financial and life planning. Two of her books, Dare 2 Dream and The Quiet Shift were awarded Third Place in the BookFest Awards and were featured on the NASDAQ billboard in New York Times Square. In addition, The Quiet Shift received the International Book Award Finalist recognition for 2023 in the category Health: Aging/50+ and it won the inaugural Literary Global Book Award in the category Health: Aging/50+.

Her commitment to financial education and planning was recognized as she was named Investopedia's Top 100 Independent Financial Advisors for 2022 and 2023, Investment News Hot 100 for 2023 while also being recognized with The Investment News Woman to Watch

Trailblazer of the Year Finalist and an honorable mention by Invest in Others as Trailblazer of the Year in 2023. She released her strategic leadership guidebook in November 2023 titled Out of the Woods, Put Some Respect on Our Names with her sister. In December 2023, she was featured again on the New York Times Square billboard for her many accomplishments.

Nicole earned a Doctorate in Transformational Leadership with top honors from Boston University, an M.Div. Magna Cum Laude from New Brunswick Theological Seminary, and a B.S. Cum Laude from Oral Roberts University.

After thirty years of industry experience that recognizes an economic cultural reckoning is occurring, Simpson is equipped, realizing she is an anomaly and has much to contribute to the inevitable change America is demanding. This reality demands her to be available as a "teacher, trainer, mentor, guidance counselor".

Made in the USA
Middletown, DE
20 September 2024